P9-DGH-595

Presented to:

Ruth

By:

Wanda ~ Alex

Date:

Happy Birthday (06)

Proverbs 3: 5 - 6
            23, 24.

Honor Books® is an imprint of
Cook Communications Ministries, Colorado Springs, CO 80918
Cook Communications, Paris, Ontario
Kingsway Communications Ltd., Eastbourne, England

Water from the Rock: Meditations on Grace and Hope—Timeless
Writings to Strengthen Your Faith and Anchor Your Soul
© 2005 BORDON BOOKS

First Printing, 2005
Printed in the United States of America
2 3 4 5 6 Printing / Year 09 08 07 06 05

Developed by Bordon Books
Manuscript written and compiled by Christi Flagg
Designed by Keochel-Peterson and Associates

Scripture quotations marked NIV are taken from the *Holy Bible, New International
Version.* NIV®. Copyright © 1973, 1978, 1984 by International Bible Society. Used by
permission of Zondervan Publishing House. All rights reserved; KJV are taken from
the *King James Version of the Bible*; MSG are taken from *The Message*, copyright © by
Eugene H. Peterson, 1993, 1994, 1995, 1996. Used by permission of NavPress
Publishing Group; NASB are taken from the *New American Standard Bible.* Copyright ©
The Lockman Foundation 1960, 1962, 1963, 1968, 1971, 1972, 1973, 1975, 1977,
1995. Used by permission; AMP are taken from *The Amplified Bible, New Testament.*
Copyright © 1958, 1987 by the Lockman Foundation, La Habra, California. Used by
permission; *The Amplified Bible, Old Testament.* Copyright © 1965, 1987by Zonderman
Corporation, Grand Rapids, Michigan. Used by permission; NKJV are taken from *The
New King James Version.* Copyright © 1979, 1980, 1982, Thomas Nelson, Inc.; NLT are
taken from the *Holy Bible, New Living Translation,* copyright © 1996. Used by permission of Tyndale House Publishers, Inc., Wheaton, Illinois 60189. All rights reserved.

Antiquated spellings, vocabulary, and punctuation usage in the selected texts of some
of the historical writers quoted in this book have been edited to conform to present-
day American English usage so that the edited quotations will convey the same meaning to the contemporary reader that the original writers intended to express.

ISBN: 1-56292-357-9

WATER FROM THE ROCK

MEDITATIONS ON GRACE AND HOPE:

TIMELESS WRITINGS TO STRENGTHEN YOUR FAITH AND ANCHOR YOUR SOUL

HONOR HB BOOKS

Inspiration and Motivation for the Seasons of Life

COOK COMMUNICATIONS MINISTRIES
Colorado Springs, Colorado • Paris, Ontario
KINGSWAY COMMUNICATIONS LTD
Eastbourne, England

Contents

INTRODUCTION

Water from the Rock: Timeless Writings on Grace and Hope is a devotional filled with the writings of great men and women of God—writings we believe will offer you wisdom and insight as you strive to live as a Christian in this world. These entries are specifically focused on the topics of grace and hope.

We pray that your heart will be encouraged as you read excerpts from Dwight L. Moody, Charles H. Spurgeon, Hannah Whitall Smith, Annie Johnson Flint, John Wesley, John Bunyan, Evelyn Underhill, and so many more.

These timeless insights of well-known and lesser known classic Christian writers are sure to leave you better equipped to live in harmony with your Creator. And like water from a rock in the midst of the desert, we hope they will refresh your thirsty soul.

[God] split the rocks in the desert and gave them water as abundant as the seas; he brought streams out of a rocky crag and made water flow down like rivers.

PSALM 78:15-16 NIV

POWERFUL GRACE

From the fullness of his grace we have all received
one blessing after another.

JOHN 1:16 NIV

God's grace is a gift. It is given to us freely and blesses our lives. We cannot do without it, and we cannot repay it. The fourteenth-century pastor and preacher, Johannes Tauler (1300 - 1361), writes about the power of God's grace in our lives. As we spend time with Christ and are immersed in His loving grace, we become more like Him. His grace is absolving, reassuring, encouraging, and strong.

All the works which people and animals could ever accomplish without the grace of God—all of them together, however great they may be— are an absolute nothing, as compared with the smallest thing which God has worked in people by His grace. As much as God is superior to all His creatures, so much more superior are His works than all the works, or wisdom, or designs, which all people could devise. Even the smallest drop of grace is better than all earthly riches that are beneath the sun.

A drop of grace is nobler than all angels and all souls, and all the natural things that God has made. And yet grace is given more richly by God to the soul than any earthly gift. It is given more richly than brooks of water, than the breath of the air, than the brightness of the sun; for spiritual things are far finer and nobler than earthly things. The whole Trinity, Father, Son, and Holy

Ghost, give grace to the soul, and flow immediately into it. Even the highest angel, in spite of its great nobility, cannot do this.

Grace looses us from the snares of many temptations. It relieves us from the heavy burden of worldly anxieties, and carries our spirit up to heaven, the land of spirits. It kills the worm of conscience, which makes sins alive. Grace is a very powerful thing. The person who receives even a tiny drop of grace is ruined for all else.

Grace makes, contrary to nature, all sorrows sweet, and brings it about that a person no longer feels any enjoyment for things that formerly gave great pleasure and delight. On the other hand, what formerly was found to be disgusting, now delights and is the desire of the heart—for instance, weakness, sorrow, inwardness, humility, self-abandonment, and detachment from others. All of this is very dear to a person, when this visitation of the Holy Ghost—grace—has in truth come to them.

-JOHANNES TAULER

When we are feeling weak, pitiful, and tired, we have the opportunity to turn to God and pray, "Dearest Lord, I need more of Your grace. I need more of Your presence. Bless me, for I won't leave until You do." And God will bless us. He will touch us as He touched Jacob and blessed him and changed his name from Supplanter to Prince with God. (See Genesis 32:28.)

> *Marvelous, infinite, matchless grace,*
> *Freely bestowed on all who believe!*
> *You that are longing to see His face,*
> *Will you this moment His grace receive?*

-JULIA H. JOHNSTON

THE LIGHT OF HOPE

Let him who walks in the dark, who has no light, trust in the name of
the LORD and rely on his God.

ISAIAH 50:10 NIV

The hope of Christ is our light. It cuts through the darkness.
It guides us and lets us walk safely down the right path. We don't
have to fear getting lost if we continue to seek God and obey
Him.

Light shows us where to go. We don't always have enough
light to see far down the path—through forests and over mountains— but we can at least see our next step. God will always give
us direction, and when we feel like we don't know how to make
our next major life decision, we need not worry or fret. All we
have to do is keep following God and obeying Him in the little
things, and He will help us with the big things. It is as simple and
complex as trusting Him and taking baby steps.

When we feel fearful or discouraged and negative thoughts
and worries cloud our minds, all we have to do is turn to God.
Darkness and light are the same to God. (See Psalm 139:12.)
Even in the darkness, He can see the obstacles that lay ahead in
the path. As He shines His light on them, we can see them too,
and we realize that many are nothing more than phantoms—fear
and lies from Satan. Sometimes what seems like a huge monster
in the darkness is a small bug in the light.

Light also helps us see that God is much bigger than our
problems. They may be huge and out of control, but God is pow-

erful and able to handle them with ease.

God's light fills us with hope—hope that sometimes shines as brightly as the sun. These are the good days when we have no doubts. At other times, it's the warmth of a small lamp, giving us just enough light and peace to help us sleep through the night, reminded that God loves and protects us.

> [God said,] "I will lead the blind by ways they have not known, along unfamiliar paths I will guide them; I will turn the darkness into light before them and make the rough places smooth. These are the things I will do; I will not forsake them."
>
> ISAIAH 42:16 NIV

GRACE AND PEACE

Grace and peace to you from God our Father and the Lord Jesus Christ.

GALATIANS 1:3 NIV

The concept of grace is not always easy to grasp. The idea that God forgives our sins, and then gives us the power to stop sinning, is indeed an astounding one. But it is true. Through the forgiveness bought by the sacrifice of Christ and the power of the Holy Spirit, we can glorify God in our daily actions. Martin Luther (1483-1546) explains the wonder and purpose of grace and peace to each Christian soul.

The greeting of the Apostle Paul when he says, "Grace and peace to you" is amazing to people of the world. Only those who belong to Christ comprehend the two words, grace and peace. Grace releases sin, and peace makes the conscience quiet.

The two fiends that torment us are sin and conscience. But Christ has defeated these two monsters and trodden them under His foot, both in this world and in the world to come. Therefore these two words contain the whole sum of Christianity in their meaning. Grace contains the remission of sins, and peace contains a quiet and joyful conscience.

But peace of conscience can never be had, unless sin is first forgiven. But sin is not forgiven by the fulfilling of the law; for no one is able to satisfy the law. But the law shows us sin, accuses and terrifies our conscience, declares the wrath of God, and drives one to desperation.

And one cannot take away sin through the works and creations of people, like strict rules, religious practices, vows, and pilgrimages. But there is no work that can take away sin; but instead works increase sin. For the perfectionists and merit-mongers, the more they labor and sweat to bring themselves out of sin, the deeper they are plunged into it. For there is no means to take away sin, but through grace alone.

Therefore Paul, in all the greetings of his letters, sets grace and peace against sin and evil conscience. The words themselves are easy. But, it is hard to be persuaded in our hearts, that by grace alone—not by any other means either in heaven or in earth—we have remission of sins and peace with God.

-MARTIN LUTHER

We don't have to worry if we can't understand Luther's explanation of grace. All we need to remember is that God is good, and all good—or grace—flows from Him.

Wonderful grace of Jesus,
Greater than all my sin;
Taking away my burden,
Setting my spirit free.

-HALDOR LILLENAS

CHRIST, OUR HOPE

*Looking for the blessed hope and glorious appearing of
our great God and Savior Jesus Christ.*

TITUS 2:13 NKJV

Christ is our hope. We have nothing of value without Him.
Why? Christ is God in the form of a person who came and lived,
suffered, and died on earth like us. But unlike us, He rose from
the dead.

Christ's death was important for many reasons. He was the
sin offering, a pure and spotless Lamb that spilled its blood for
our sins. Since He was absolutely pure and absolutely God,
Christ's sacrifice was the last one. Before Jesus' death on the cross,
the Jewish priests had to offer yearly sacrifices to atone for the sins
of the people. After His glorious resurrection, other sacrifices
were no longer needed. (See Hebrews 7.) Our sins have been
wiped away once and for all. They are no longer keeping us from
a loving relationship with God. Christ broke down the wall of our
sins that separated us from our holy Creator. All we need do is
appropriate His sacrifice—already offered and accepted—and
our sins are covered.

But Christ isn't just our sin eraser. He's also "our living hope"
(1 Timothy 1:1 MSG). When we call upon His name and ask
Him to take over our messy lives, Christ gives us the power to
overcome sin, live as saints, and glorify God with our actions. And
when we turn our lives over to Him, we will find peace, we will
find joy, and we will discover what we've always wanted— hope.

Christ is God; He made us. He knows us intimately, and He loves us. He knows what will give us joy—not just what will make us temporarily happy, but what will give us a complete joy. Christ said, "These things I have spoken to you, that My joy may remain in you, and that your joy may be full" (John 15:11 NKJV).

May our joy and hope be full in Christ!

Though now you do not see Him, yet believing,
you rejoice with joy inexpressible.

1 PETER 1:8 NKJV

ALL SHALL BE WELL!

*[God] shall wipe away every tear from their eyes;
and there shall no longer be any death; there shall no longer be any
mourning, or crying, or pain.*

There are times when we don't understand why the world is
full of hatred and strife, or why we ourselves have a past—and
sometimes a present— full of that same inability to love and get
along with others. We wish sin had never entered the world.
Julian of Norwich (1342-1416) felt that same frustration with
herself and the world. The answer God spoke to her heart as she
prayed is a comforting message to all those who torment themselves with regret or wonder how God will manage to make good
come out of so much evil in the world.

After this the Lord brought to my mind the longing that I
had for Him before. And I saw that nothing prevented me [from
coming to Him] but sin. And I thought: If sin had not been, we
should all have been clean and like to our Lord, as He made us.
And thus, in my folly, before this time often I wondered why by
the great foreseeing wisdom of God the beginning of sin was not
prevented: for then, I thought, all should have been well.

This inner turmoil was much to be forsaken, but nevertheless
I made mourning and sorrow because of it, without reason and
discretion. But Jesus, who in this Vision informed me of all that is

needful to me, answered: "It is necessary that there should be sin; but all shall be well."

These words were said quite tenderly, showing no manner of blame to me nor to any who would be saved. So it would be a great unkindness to blame or wonder at God for my sin, since He doesn't blame me. And in these words I saw a marvelous high mystery hidden in God, which mystery He shall openly make known to us in Heaven: then we shall truly see why He suffered sin to come. In sight of this, we shall have endless joy in our Lord God.

-JULIAN OF NORWICH

Sometimes we must trust in the good God who knows all, rather than go on in fear of the things we don't understand. Rest in His goodness today in spite of questions still unanswered and insight yet incomplete.

GRACE AND PRAYER

Be devoted to one another in brotherly love; . . . rejoicing in hope,
persevering in tribulation, devoted to prayer.

ROMANS 12:10,12 NASB

Often after a busy day of preaching and healing, Jesus escaped
for alone time with God. Mark mentions that He "went off to a
solitary place, where he prayed" (Mark 1:35 niv). Jesus was able to
be full of love and grace because of this time with the Father. We
can be too! Walter Hilton (1340-1396), a fourteenth-century
priest, writes that prayer is a channel for grace between us and
God.

Prayer is fast and profitable when we use it to gain purity of
heart by destroying sin and accepting virtues. We don't have to
pray for the purpose of making our Lord know what we desire,
for He knows well enough what we need.

Instead prayer is used to make us ready and able, as clean ves-
sels, to receive the grace which our Lord would freely give us.
Grace cannot be felt until we are strengthened and purified by the
fire of desire in devout prayer.

Although prayer does not cause our Lord to give us grace,
nevertheless it is a way by which grace freely given comes into our
soul.

-WALTER HILTON

Grace taught my soul to pray
And made mine eyes o'erflow;
'Twas grace which kept me to this day,
And will not let me go.

-PHILLIP DODDRIDGE

Through the communion with Christ in prayer, our hearts break open wide to receive what He died to give us.

SEEK GOD CONTINUALLY

Lead me in Thy truth and teach me, for Thou art the God
of my salvation; for Thee I wait all the day.

PSALM 25:5 NASB

Sometimes all we need as Christians is the hope to keep
going, to keep helping others, to keep believing that God's good
will win out, and to keep seeking God in our own lives. Augustine
of Hippo (354-430) offers this prayer for God, who is our hope,
to give us hope to keep seeking and relying on Him.

O Lord, my God, I believe in You, Father, Son, and Holy
Spirit. In as much as I can, in as much as You have given me the
power, I have sought You. I became weary and I labored.

O Lord my God, my sole hope, help me to believe and never
to cease seeking You. Grant that I may always and ardently seek
out Your countenance. Give me the strength to seek You, for You
help me to find You and You have more and more given me the
hope of finding You.

Here I am before You with my determination and my frailty.
Preserve the first and heal the second. Here I am before You with
my strength and my ignorance. Where You have opened the door
to me, welcome me at the entrance; where You have closed the
door to me, open to my cry; enable me to remember You, to
understand You, and to love You. Amen.

-AUGUSTINE OF HIPPO

O God, You are altogether lovely. You continuously bless us and take care of us. You seek us when we are lost and give us strength and courage and love when we run out of our own. Let us daily remember Your love, and learn to rest in Your presence more and more. Amen

In sweet communion, Lord, with Thee
I constantly abide;
My hand Thou holdest in Thy own
To keep me near Thy side.

-WILLIAM U. BUTCHER

GRACE AND LOVE

What marvelous love the Father has extended to us! Just look at it—
we're called children of God! . . . But friends, that's exactly who we are:
children of God. And that's only the beginning. Who knows how we'll
end up! What we know is that when Christ is openly revealed, we'll see
him—and in seeing him, become like him.

1 JOHN 3:1-2 MSG

God's love and grace dwell in our hearts as soon as we call on
Jesus to be our Lord and ask His Spirit into our lives. Once God
lives in us, and we live in Him by reading His Word and praying,
we become more holy and loving every day. Henry Scougal (1650-
1678) writes that love and good deeds in a holy person's life is not
just a strict way of life, but a natural outpouring of God's love.

The love and goodness which a reverent person bears for God
is not by a command forcing them so to do, but rather a new
nature instructing and prompting them to it. They don't pay their
devotions as an unavoidable tribute only to appease divine justice
or to quiet their loud conscience; but those religious exercises are
the proper emanations of the divine life, the natural enjoyment of
the newborn soul.

They pray, and give thanks, and repent, not only because these
things are commanded, but rather because they are sensible of
their wants, and of the divine goodness, and of the folly and mis-
ery of a sinful life. Their love and kindness is not forced, and their

offerings are not forced from them. Their love makes them willing to give. Injustice or greed, and all other vices, are as contrary to their temper and constitution, as the basest actions are to the most generous spirit, and disrespect and vulgarity to those who are naturally modest.

So that I may well say with John, "Whoever has been born of God does not sin, for His seed remains in him; and he cannot sin, because he has been born of God" (1 John 3:9 NKJV). Though holy and religious people do often read the law of God, and have a great regard for it, yet it is not so much the principle of the law, as its reasonableness, and purity, and goodness, which do succeed with them. They account it excellent and desirable in itself, and that in keeping of it there is great reward; and that divine love in which they are moved, makes them become a law unto themselves.

-HENRY SCOUGAL

An example of the natural love Henry Scougal describes would be when parents love and care for a small child. The child naturally loves them in return and brings them bits of food, toys, and samples of their artwork. The child talks constantly of their parents to others, bragging with excitement at how big, how smart, and how strong they are.

We can be just as excited when talking of our Heavenly Father. He enjoys our gifts, and He loves to hear our praise and our thanks the same way we enjoy hearing our children speak of their love for us.

HOPE IN AN UNSEEN GOD

[Jesus said,] "The sheep listen to his voice.
He calls his own sheep by name and leads them out.
When he has brought out all his own, he goes on ahead of them,
and his sheep follow him because they know his voice."

JOHN 10:3-4 NIV

We often find it hard to put our trust in an invisible God. It's difficult to have hope for the future because we can't see Him clearly. Dwight L. Moody (1837-1899) gives the perfect example of knowing God's voice and responding to it, even when we can't see Him.

I had been absent from home for some days, and was wondering, as I again drew near the house, if my little Maggie, just able to sit alone, would remember me. To test her memory, I stationed myself where I could not be seen by her, and called her name in the familiar tone, "Maggie!" She dropped her toys, glanced around the room, and then looked down upon them.

Again I repeated her name, "Maggie," and she once more surveyed the room. But when she didn't see her father's face, she looked very sad, and slowly resumed her playing. Once more I called, "Maggie!" and, dropping her toys, and bursting into tears, she stretched out her arms in the direction where the sound came from, knowing that, though she could not see him, her father must be there for she knew his voice.

-DWIGHT L. MOODY

When God speaks, we will recognize His voice. It is the still, small voice Elijah heard, and we will hear when we wait for Him. It will always agree with Scripture, encourage us, and lead us to good.

[God] said, "Go out, and stand on the mountain before the LORD." And behold, the LORD passed by, and a great and strong wind tore into the mountains and broke the rocks in pieces before the LORD, but the LORD was not in the wind; and after the wind an earthquake, but the LORD was not in the earthquake; and after the earthquake a fire, but the LORD was not in the fire; and after the fire a still small voice. So it was, when Elijah heard it, that he wrapped his face in his mantle and went out and stood in the entrance of the cave.

1 KINGS 19:11-13 NKJV

AUTOMATIC
DISCIPLINES OF GRACE

At the time, discipline isn't much fun. It always feels like
it's going against the grain. Later, of course, it pays off handsomely,
for it's the well-trained who find themselves mature
in their relationship with God.

HEBREWS 12:11 MSG

Musicians, artists, and athletes spend hours of their lives each day working out, playing scales, and improving their talent. And after they perform, run a race, or display their work, nobody questions the time and energy they spent. Nobody says, "You gave up so much. Was it really worth it?" to someone like Lance Armstrong, Maya Angelou, or Yo Yo Ma. They think instead, *If I had that ability, I would spend hours each day practicing.*

Some people go through years of training and give up all kinds of things for the reward of a developed talent, and they and others think it is well worth the sacrifice. How much more should we be willing to give up for the glorious promises of God?

Discipline for discipline's sake is meaningless, but discipline for a life closer to God is worth the effort. The Christian disciplines encouraged in church and in the Bible aren't designed to clutter our lives with activity or to make us give up all that we consider fun; instead, they are there to strengthen our spiritual muscles and give us the ability to lean on God more and more.

Oswald Chambers (1874-1917) reminds us that although God's grace gives us the initial ability to tap into His presence and His power, it is our daily practicing that keeps us standing in the storms of life.

The question of forming habits on the basis of the grace of God is a vital one. To ignore it is to fall into the snare of the Pharisee—the grace of God is praised, Jesus Christ is praised, the Redemption is praised, but the practical everyday life evades working out. If we refuse to practice, it is not God's grace that fails when a crisis comes, but our own nature.

If we will obey the Spirit of God and practice through our physical life all that God has put in our hearts by His Spirit, then when the crisis comes we shall find that we have not only God's grace to stand by us but our own nature also. And when the crisis has passed without any disaster, but exactly the opposite happens, the soul is built up into a stronger attitude towards God.[1]

-OSWALD CHAMBERS

In order to find grace through Christian discipline, we must remember that discipline is intended to strengthen us. It motivates us to listen carefully for God's voice and hear and respond when He speaks.

"The reason you practice so much is so that you will do things automatically the same way every time."

-DR. WILLIAM C. DEVRIES

WHEN THERE IS NO HOPE

Though the fig tree may not blossom, nor fruit be on the vines; . . .
Though the flock may be cut off from the fold, and there be no herd in
the stalls—Yet I will rejoice in the LORD, I will joy in the God of my
salvation.

HABAKKUK 3:17-18 NKJV

There seems to be an expectation of Christians to be shiny,
happy people who don't make mistakes, have no major problems,
and for whom God smoothes the way so their lives are easy. This
isn't true. A quick glance at the life of Jesus or the early disciples
or even the Old Testament prophets proves that a life following
God isn't simple. But it is full of joy.

Although her best-selling book was titled *The Christian's Secret
of a Happy Life*, Hannah Whitall Smith (1832-1911) did not have
an easy life herself. She writes of rejoicing in God in spite of difficulties and discouragement and discovering that beyond everything, there was still God.

There come times in many lives, when the soul finds itself
without any comfort both outward and inward. When all seems
dark, and all seems wrong. When everything in which we have
trusted seems to fail us. When the promises are apparently unful-
filled, and our prayers gain no response. When there seems nothing left to rest on in earth or Heaven.

The soul must wade through the swamp, and fall off of the cliff, and be swamped by the ocean, and at last find in the midst of them, and at the bottom of them, and behind them, the present, living, loving, omnipotent God! And then, and not until then, will it understand the prophet's exulting shout of triumph, and be able to join it: "Yet I will rejoice in the LORD, I will joy in the God of my salvation."

All of God's saints in all ages have done this. Job said, out of the depths of sorrow and trial which few can equal, "Though He slay me, yet will I trust Him" (Job 13:15 NKJV). David could say in the moment of his strongest anguish, "Yea, though I walk through the valley of the shadow of death," yet "I will fear no evil; for You are with me" (Psalm 23:4 NKJV).

-HANNAH WHITALL SMITH

O God, thank You for being our hope when there is no hope. Give us courage and faith to rejoice when things go wrong because You will never go wrong. We can have joy in You no matter what.

"It's a good thing to have all the props pulled out from under us occasionally. It gives us some sense of what is rock under our feet, and what is sand."

-MADELEINE L'ENGLE

REMEMBER THE HOPE OF GOD

By your words I can see where I'm going;
they throw a beam of light on my dark path.

PSALM 119:105 MSG

Sometimes we have a hard time following God and knowing which way to go. We feel frozen and stuck in the dark, unable to find our way out or to hear God's voice.

The first thing to do is to start reading the Psalms. God's Word is our hope and the light on our dark path. Read it aloud. It helps. David and the other Psalm writers weren't afraid to tell God what they were feeling, how scared they were, how angry they were, how lonely they were. If you read along with their words, you, too, will be able to share with God your fears and experiences.

The second thing to do, once you are fed with God's Word, is to be sure to do what you felt God last told you to. Many times God won't speak if we've ignored the last thing He told us. God often tells us something to do or gives us a word of encouragement before the dark times come.

If we cling tightly to God and what He has said, we will either stay with Him or keep going with Him and find ourselves in the light of His hope during and after our struggles.

Don't forget in the darkness
what you have learned in the light.

-JOE BAYLY

GRACE AND GENTLENESS TO OTHERS

[Jesus said,] "Don't pick on people, jump on their failures,
criticize their faults—unless, of course, you want the same treatment.
Don't condemn those who are down; that hardness can boomerang.
Be easy on people; you'll find life a lot easier."

LUKE 6:37 MSG

Followers of Christ are not perfect. They aren't even naturally nicer or better people than others. However, they are aware of their weaknesses and imperfections. This awareness causes two things: a dependence on Christ for grace and strength and a graceful and gentle spirit toward other sinners. It is this forgiving spirit that Evelyn Underhill (1850-1941) focuses on. She reminds us that our patience and love toward others' sins opens the channel of grace from God as He forgives us.

If a repentant Christian dares to ask that their many departures from the Christian norm, their impatience, gloom, self-occupation, unloving prejudices, reckless tongue, feverish desires, with all the damage they have caused to Christ's Body, be set aside, because, in spite of all, they long for God and Eternal Life: then they must set aside and forgive all of the impatience, selfishness, bitter and foolish speech, and sudden yieldings to base impulse that others have caused them to endure.

Hardness is the one impossible thing. Harshness to others in those who ask and need the mercy of God sets up a conflict at the very heart of personality and shuts the door upon grace.

-EVELYN UNDERHILL

[Jesus said,] "In prayer there is a connection between what God does and what you do. You can't get forgiveness from God, for instance, without also forgiving others. If you refuse to do your part, you cut yourself off from God's part."

MATTHEW 6:14-15 MSG

HOPE AND TRUST

Blessed is the man who trusts in the LORD,
And whose hope is the LORD.

JEREMIAH 17:7 NKJV

When our faith is as simple as a child's, God will not let us down. When we trust and wait on Him, He loves to provide. The following story by the evangelist Charles Finney (1792-1875) is an example of how God will provide and feed His children, when they trust and hope in Him.

I found in Syracuse a Christian woman who was called Mother Austin, a woman of most remarkable faith. She was poor and entirely dependent on the charity of the people.

I do not think I ever witnessed greater faith in its simplicity than the faith this woman manifested. She said to me on one occasion, "Brother Finney, it is impossible for me to suffer for any of the necessities of life, because God has said to me, 'Trust (lean on, rely on, and be confident) in the LORD and do good; so shall you dwell in the land and feed surely on His faithfulness, and truly you shall be fed'" (Psalm 37:3 AMP).

One Saturday evening a friend of hers, an unrepentant man, called to see her. After talking awhile with her, he offered her a five-dollar bill as he was leaving. She felt an inward nudge not to take it because she felt that it would be an act of self-righteousness on the part of that man, and it might do him more harm than it would do her good. She therefore declined to take it, and he went away. She had just enough wood and food in the house to last through Sunday, and that was all.

On Sunday there came a violent snowstorm. She had a young son who lived with her. They arose on Monday morning and found themselves snowed in on every side. They found enough fuel for a little fire, and soon the boy began to ask what they would have for breakfast. She said, "I do not know, my son, but the LORD will provide."

She looked out, and nobody could pass through the streets. The boy began to weep bitterly and concluded that they would freeze and starve to death. However, she set her table, believing that breakfast would come at the right time.

Very soon she heard a loud talking in the street and went to the window to see what it was. Several men were outside, shoveling the snow so that a horse could get through. They came up to her door; and when she opened it, she saw that they had brought her plenty of fuel and food, everything to make her comfortable for several days.

It was well-known throughout the city that Mother Austin's faith was like a bank. She never suffered for lack of the necessities of life because she drew on God.

-CHARLES FINNEY

God is so good. He loves to rescue us and remind us of His grace and mercy. Even though Mother Austin's son gave up hope, God provided food and warmth for him along with his mother. And through this provision, he was taught how compassionate and faithful God is. Let us remember the times God has provided, and may these memories give us hope for His provision in the future.

HOPE IN GOD'S GRACE

God has actually given us his Spirit (not the world's spirit) so we can know the wonderful things God has freely given us.

1 CORINTHIANS 2:12 NLT

Sometimes when all is dark, extremely dark, I would be overwhelmed in grief and despair if I looked at the outward appearance of things. At these times I seek to encourage myself in God. I grab a hold in faith on His almighty power, His unchangeable love, and His infinite wisdom.

I say to myself, "God is able and willing to deliver me, if it is good for me. For it is written, 'He who did not spare His own Son, but delivered Him up for us all, how shall He not with Him also freely give us all things?'" (Romans 8:32 NKJV). When I believe this through grace, it keeps my soul in peace.

-GEORGE MÜLLER

Wide, wide as the ocean, high as the Heaven above;
Deep, deep as the deepest sea is my Savior's love.

-C. AUSTIN MILES

THE GRACE OF CHRIST'S LOVE

Grace mixed with faith and love poured over me and into me. And all because of Jesus.

1 TIMOTHY 1:14 MSG

God doesn't only give us His love and acceptance for us; He gives us His love for others. When Joanna P. Moore (1832-1916) started a home for elderly freed slave women in New Orleans, she struggled with having and showing Christ's love each day. She prayed repeatedly for the gift to love those she served, and God answered with His grace.

I must refer to a lesson I learned in this home, and one I have to review daily or I forget it. It is this: You must love before you can comfort and help.

I've told you how repulsive most of these old people I cared for were to me. God showed me that I only pitied them. I did not love them, as Christ loved me when I was all covered with sin and was in rebellion against Him. I did not love even to shake their hands, and yet I would have shared my last piece of bread with them. I knew this feeling was wrong and spent many hours in prayer asking for a baptism of love.

One night I received the answer to my prayer. The next morning we rang the bell as usual for prayers and the old people came tottering in. Our lesson was Luke 23:27-45. I read the comforting words of Jesus to the weeping women with tears in my voice, and when I came to: "Father, forgive them; for they know not what they do," (verse 34 KJV) we all burst into tears and fell on our knees and prayed.

After prayer the old people gathered around me saying, "Sister Moore, we will not worry you any more. We'll be good." They saw they could put their arms around me, and I let them, for my heart was full of love. After this it was easier for me to work with and help them. I did not need to say in words that I loved them. They read in the touch of my hand and the tone of my voice.

O, God, I long to be always full of this overflowing love of God—a love that all the coldness and ingratitude of earth cannot chill.

-JOANNA P. MOORE

Father, make us loving, gentle, thoughtful, kind;
Fill us with Thy Spirit, make us of Thy mind.
Help us love each other, more and more each day,
Help us follow Jesus, in the narrow way.

-FLORA KIRKLAND

CULTIVATING PATIENCE AND HOPE

We pray that you'll have the strength to stick it out over the long haul—not the grim strength of gritting your teeth but the glory—strength God gives. It is strength that endures the unendurable and spills over into joy, thanking the Father who makes us strong enough to take part in everything bright and beautiful that he has for us.

COLOSSIANS 1:11-12 MSG

True patience is based firmly on God's hope. This hope does spill over with joy while we are in the midst of our trials, rather than waiting until they are over to rejoice. This patience doesn't come all at once either.

Patience is a virtue that usually grows slowly. For the Christian, patience is based on trust, faith, and humility. We trust that God is in control of our lives. We have faith that His purpose for us is good. And we are humble and willing to suffer in the present, knowing we will be blessed in the future.

Patience is based on and gets its strength from hope, a stubborn and active hope. This hope is strong enough to hold onto the goodness and the promises of God in the face of large problems and persistent pain.

Now God cultivates this hope by repeatedly answering prayer and blessing us when our problems seem too great. The repeated pattern is: We face problems, we feel scared, we pray, we decide to hang in there for at least one more day, and then God answers our prayers by either fixing the problems or by giving us the strength and peace to make it through them. When God has answered our cry for help, our hope and our patience grow as our trust and faith in Him increases.

Let us ask God for the strength and the hope to make it through the problems in this world. May He bless us with His peace that covers and comforts all our worries and fears.

"Soon my prayers were answered, first when patience miraculously descended like soft chick-yellow parachute silk. . . . But patience is when God—or something—makes the now a little roomier."

-ANNE LAMOTT

GOD'S GRACE IN THE INCARNATION

Of His fullness, we have all received, and grace upon grace.
For the Law was given through Moses;
grace and truth were realized through Jesus Christ.

JOHN 1:16-17 NASB

Can we as Christians be perfect? On one hand, we have the Holy Spirit living inside of us and giving us power to do "greater things" than Christ. (See John 14:12.) But on the other hand, we have to remain aware of our human weakness and rely on God for our strength. We tend to get distracted and think we don't need Christ's help all the time. But Christ was human and God in one. He didn't sin although He was tempted. St. Augustine explores how Christ, the perfection of God, can inhabit a human form.

Why should there be such great glory in one of human nature? This is undoubtedly an act of grace. No obvious merit comes from having Christ in the form of a human except that those who consider such a question faithfully and soberly would have here a clear demonstration of God's great grace. Then they might understand how they themselves are justified from their sins by the same grace, which made it so that the human Christ had no power to sin.

Therefore the angel hailed His mother when announcing to

her the future birth: "Hail," he said, "full of grace." And he said short-ly after, "You have found favor with God." And it was said of her, that she was full of grace, since she was to be mother of her LORD, indeed the LORD of all.

Yet, concerning Christ himself, when the Evangelist John said, "And the Word became flesh and dwelt among us," he added, "and we beheld His glory, the glory as of the only begotten of the Father, full of grace and truth" (John 1:14 NKJV). When he said, "The Word became flesh," this means "Full of grace." And when he said, "The glory of the only begotten of the Father," this means "Full of truth."

Indeed it was Truth himself, God's only begotten Son—and, again, this not by grace but by nature—who, by grace, assumed human nature into such a personal unity that He himself became the Son of Man as well.

-AUGUSTINE OF HIPPO

As we put our trust in Christ who was sinless on this earth, we will be more and more open to His grace and able to be perfect and full of love like Him.

"Neither does Christ give grace and peace, as the Apostles gave and brought the same unto men by preaching of the Gospel; but he gives it as the Author and Creator. The Father creates and gives life, grace, peace, and all other good things. The self-same things also the Son creates and gives."

-MARTIN LUTHER

HOPE IN SPITE OF HURT

Jesus said, "Father, forgive them, for
they do not know what they do."

LUKE 23:34 NKJV

That Christ forgave, first Judas who betrayed Him, and then the crowd of Jews who demanded His death and the Roman soldiers who crucified Him, is a miracle of love. His compassion was so great that, at the highest point of pain and abandonment by God, Christ asked for our forgiveness. The modern Quaker, Douglas Steere, writes of this forgiving love as proof that Jesus could only be God.

The capacity of Jesus to forgive another, and to reenter vulnerably into the deepest relation with another, is the strongest evidence of his being God in the flesh. For only so could someone be truly able to forgive others.

This vulnerability of love relationships is a struggle for all of us. We have emotions and desire love, understanding, and friendship, but to receive them we must open up and chance being hurt by rejection or abandonment. Many of us decide love isn't worth it, and we close off the sensitive center of our hearts. Others are disappointed by a friend, so we dump that person and turn to the next relationship hoping that it will save us. We get hurt over and over until eventually we become broken, cynical people.

But God designed us to forgive. He forgave us when we rejected Him, our Creator, our Father, our LORD. And His forgiveness can flow through us to forgive others. Just as the old saying goes, "It is better to have loved and lost, than to never have loved at all," it also is better to remain vulnerable as children, because then we have a chance for childish joy and delight.

Our goal should be to open up to, forgive, and love others, but to keep our hope in God. God alone will never disappoint. There may be times when we feel abandoned or hurt by God, but if we continue to pour ourselves into Him and confess and even yell at Him for our hurt, He will always respond with love, compassion, and His presence.

God adores us. Just as we don't want to see our children cold and cynical, doubting our love, obeying our rules but not trusting whether we will feed and take care of them, God doesn't want us to distrust Him or view Him as a cruel dictator who doesn't care. If a child confronts his or her parents saying, "You don't love me, you think I'm a burden, and I can't do anything right!" the parents will respond in shock and then in love, reassuring the child of their love, care, and enjoyment of them.

Jesus is the key to forgiveness and vulnerability. And vulnerability is the key to hope, to joy, and to love.

-DOUGLAS STEERE

"When we were children, we used to think that when we were grown up we would no longer be vulnerable. But to grow up is to accept vulnerability. . . . To be alive is to be vulnerable."

-MADELEINE L'ENGLE

NEW EVERY MORNING

GOD's loyal love couldn't have run out, his merciful love couldn't have dried up. They're created new every morning. How great your faithfulness! I'm sticking with GOD (I say it over and over). He's all I've got left.

LAMENTATIONS 3:22-24 MSG

God overflows with grace and blessings for us. His grace and love are new every morning. And we need God's love every morning. Andrew Murray (1828-1917) instructs us how to daily pray and be filled with God's grace as we spend time with Him.

The main need in our Christian life is fellowship with God. The holy life within us comes from God, and is entirely dependent on Him. As we every moment need fresh air to breathe and as the sun every moment sends down its new light, so it is only in direct living communication with God that our souls can be strong.

In Exodus, the manna of one day was rotten by the next day. We must every day have fresh grace from heaven, and we obtain it only in direct waiting upon God himself. Begin each day by waiting before God, and letting Him touch you. Take time to meet God.

Let your first act in your devotion be setting yourself still before God. In prayer, or worship, everything depends upon God taking the main place. We must bow quietly before Him in humble faith and adoration, speaking like this within our hearts: "God is. God is near. God is love; God is longing to communicate himself to me. God the Almighty One, who works all in all, is even now waiting to work in me, and make himself known." Take the time, until you know God is very near.

When you have given God His place of honor, glory, and power, take your place of deepest submission, and seek to be filled with the Spirit of humility. As people, it is our blessing to be nothing so that God may be all in us. As sinners we are not worthy to look up to God so we bow in self-abasement. As saints, we let God's love overwhelm us, and then we bow lower down still. Sink down before Him in humility, meekness, patience, and surrender to His goodness and mercy. He will exalt you. "He will lift you up" (James 4:10 NIV).

-ANDREW MURRAY

O Lord, let Your grace flow to us and remind us to turn to You moment by moment during our busy and troubled lives. We need You for Your love, for Your peace, for Your joy, but mostly for yourself. Lift us up to You as we bow down and wait at Your feet. Amen.

"Constant prayer will only 'burden' us as wings burden the bird in flight."

-DALLAS WILLARD

FREE GRACE

God who did not spare His own Son, but delivered Him over for us all,
how will He not also with Him freely give us all things?

ROMANS 8:32 NASB

God loves us so much that He gives us the freedom to accept
or reject His love. He values our choice to love Him and spend
time with Him. And once we make that choice, each time we sit
in His presence we will experience His life-changing grace. We
become more like Him, and we desire more and more of His love.
John Wesley (1703-1791) explores the free nature of God's grace
that blesses us over and over.

The grace or love of God, which gives our salvation, is free in
all. It is free in all to whom it is given.

It does not depend on any power or merit in people; no, not
in any degree, neither in whole, nor in part. It does not in any way
depend either on the good works or righteousness of the receiver;
not on anything they have done, or anything they are. It does not
depend on their endeavors. It does not depend on their good personality, or good desires, or good purposes and intentions; for all
these flow from the free grace of God; they are the streams only,
not the fountain. They are the fruits of free grace, and not the
root. They are not the cause, but the effects of it.

Whatever is good in man, or is done by man, God is the
author and doer of it. Thus is His grace free in all. That is, it is in

no way depending on any power or merit in us, but on God alone, who freely gave us His own Son, and "with Him freely gives us all things."

-JOHN WESLEY

> *Fountain of grace, rich, full and free,*
> *What need I, that is not in Thee?*
> *Full pardon, strength to meet the day,*
> *And peace which none can take away.*

-JAMES EDMESTON

THE DIFFERENCE BETWEEN KNOWLEDGE AND HOPE

Faith is being sure of what we hope for and certain of what we do not see.

HEBREWS 11:1 NIV

Hope can be anything from a slight desire for something, all the way to a firm belief in receiving it. The hope in the Bible is a firm belief. It is different from the current definition of hope, which is wishy-washy and more like "pipe dreams" and false optimism. The hope of the Bible is knowledge—a firm, unshakable knowing that changes our actions and our emotions. Dwight L. Moody emphasizes the confidence of Paul's hope and trust in Christ.

Confidence breathes through Paul's last words to Timothy: "That is why I am suffering as I am. Yet I am not ashamed, because I know whom I have believed, and am convinced that he is able to guard what I have entrusted to him for that day" (2 Timothy 1:12 NIV).

It is not a matter of doubt, but of knowledge. "I know." "I am persuaded." The word "Hope" is not used in the Scripture to express doubt. It is used in regard to the second coming of Christ, or to the resurrection of the body.

We do not say that we "hope" we are Christians. I do not say that I "hope" I am an American, or that I "hope" I am a married man. These are settled things.

I may say that I "hope" to go back to my home; or I "hope" to attend such a meeting. I do not say that I "hope" to come to this country, for I am here. And so, if we are born of God we know it; and He will not leave us in darkness if we search the Scriptures.

-DWIGHT L. MOODY

If you are worried because you only hope you are a Christian, and you hope your soul is secure in Christ, then read the Bible as Moody suggests, earnestly pray to God, and do not let go until you get an answer. God desires to convince you of His love for you and of His saving power that will change your life.

OUR VICTORY
IS ASSURED

Jesus said, "I have told you all this so that you may have peace in me.
Here on earth you will have many trials and sorrows.
But take heart, because I have overcome the world."

JOHN 16:33 NLT

In the book *Where Is God When It Hurts*, Philip Yancey says
that hope is slogging through a battle with the victory assured.
He quotes Henry Boer who said of World War II, "I never met
an enlisted man who doubted for a moment the outcome of the
war. Nor did I ever meet a marine who asked why, if victory was
so sure, we couldn't have it immediately. It was just a question of
slogging through till the enemy gave up."

That is exactly what we as Christians are doing. We live on
earth, knowing that God is in charge, but because earth is a fallen
place, people have the power to sin and hurt others. As
Christians, we also have power over evil, and Satan cannot touch
us. "The God-begotten are also the God-protected. The Evil One
can't lay a hand on them" (1 John 5:18 MSG).

The hope of God is a victorious hope. We have victory knowing that once we turn to Christ, we will live in heaven and enjoy
God's uninterrupted presence. We also have victorious hope for
the present because with Christ we have power over sin. When

He died on the cross, our sins were washed away, and when He rose again, we gained the ability to sin less and less as we spend more time with Him.

We indeed have the victory in Christ. If we remember that the war was already won, we can trust God to protect us as we step out in the next battle.

Everyone born of God overcomes the world. This is the victory that has overcome the world.

1 JOHN 5:4 NIV

STRENGTHENING TRUST

Every desirable and beneficial gift comes out of heaven. The gifts are rivers of light cascading down from the Father of Light. There is nothing deceitful in God, nothing two-faced, nothing fickle.

JAMES 1:17 MSG

How do we build our trust in someone? We spend time with that person. We get to know them, ask questions, and see if there is any contradiction in their actions or character. Soon, if things go well, we trust them with our confidence. And then, when they haven't hurt us, but desired only our good, we trust them with our love. It is the same with our faith or trust in God. We cannot build our trust in God without learning about Him, spending time with Him, and building a relationship with Him. George Müller (1805-1898) says the first step to knowing God is reading His Word.

Through reading of the Bible, and especially through meditation of it, we become more and more acquainted with the nature and character of God. We then see more and more what a kind, loving, gracious, merciful, mighty, wise, and faithful being He is. When we recognize this, we know that in poverty, in suffering, in grief, in struggles with our service, and when we are without a job, we will rest on the ability of God to help us.

We have not only learned from His Word that He has almighty power and infinite wisdom, but we have also seen many examples in the Bible where His almighty power and infinite wisdom have been actually used in helping and delivering His people. We can rest on the willingness of God to help us. We haven't only learned from the Bible what a kind, good, merciful, gracious, and faithful being God is, but we have also read in the Bible, how in many different ways He has proved Himself to be so.

When we consider that God has become known to us through prayer and meditation on His own Word, it will lead us with a measure of confidence to rely on Him and therefore will be one way for God to strengthen our faith.

-GEORGE MÜLLER

HOPE IN WEAKNESS

I would have lost heart, unless I had believed that I would see the good-ness of the LORD in the land of the living.

PSALM 27:13 NKJV

There is a hope that comes only in weakness and despair. Often we have no knowledge of our need of God when things go smoothly. It is when problems arise and threaten to overcome us, that we suddenly realize how utterly hopeless we are without Him. And yet, it is when we acknowledge our helplessness, that God is freed to take over. He is our hope. John Bunyan (1628-1688) reminds us that God's hope is saving hope, the hope of our salvation.

Hope is the grace that relieves the soul when it is dark and weary. True hope, in the right exercise of it upon God, has no problem with weakness or darkness; but rather strengthens the soul to stay in spite of and because of them. Therefore Abraham's hope was made by his weakness. (See Romans 4:18.) And the same for Paul, who said, "That is why, for Christ's sake, I delight in weaknesses, in insults, in hardships, in persecutions, in difficul-ties. For when I am weak, then I am strong" (2 Corinthians 12:10 NIV). But this cannot be done where there is no hope, nor by any-thing but hope. For it is hope, and the use of it, that can say, "Now I expect that God should bring good out of all this."

"But hope that is seen is not hope" (Romans 8:24 NKJV). But we must hope for what we don't see. David said, "Why are you cast down, O my soul? ... Hope in God" (Psalm 42:5 NKJV). Christians have no reason to mistrust the goodness of God, because of their weakness. The Psalmist said, "I would have despaired unless I had believed that I would see" (Psalm 27:13 NASB). By believing, they mean hoping to see.

There are several temptations that if hope is not in use, cannot be mastered, especially if the soul is in great and sore trials. There is irritation and impatience, there is fear and despair, and there is doubting and misunderstanding God's present work. All of these will take control if hope is not stirring; nor can any other grace put a stop to their tumultuous raging in the soul.

But now, hope in God makes all turmoil hush, and lays the soul at the foot of God.

-JOHN BUNYAN

Hope alone will keep our spirits up and fill us with energy to keep going. But it is only a hope in Christ that will sustain and fulfill our soul.

> While pilgrims here we journey on
> In this dark vale of sin and gloom,
> Till our returning King shall come
> To take His exiled captives home,
> O! what can buoy the spirits up?
> 'Tis this alone—the blessèd hope.

-ANNIE R. SMITH

IN DUE TIME CHRIST DIED FOR THE UNGODLY

God put his love on the line for us by offering his Son in sacrificial death while we were of no use whatever to him.

ROMANS 5:8 MSG

Just as children are "of no use" to their parents, we are "of no use" to God. However, the following is also true: Just as parents love and cherish their children, so God loves and cherishes us. Charles Spurgeon (1834-1892) writes to encourage those Christians who have a hard time focusing their thoughts on God and in prayer. He reminds them that God will help them in their weakness.

Some people say, "I do not seem to have strength to collect my thoughts, and keep them fixed upon the important subjects which concern my salvation. A short prayer is almost too much for me."

Note this! If you are without strength in this area, there are many like you. They could not carry out a train of consecutive thought to save their lives. Many poor men and women are illiterate and untrained, and find deep thought to be very heavy work.

You need not, therefore, despair. Continuous thought is not necessary for salvation, but instead a simple reliance upon Jesus. Hold on to this one fact—"In due time Christ died for the ungodly." (See Romans 5:8.) This truth will not require from you any deep research or profound reasoning, or convincing argument.

There it stands: "In due time Christ died for the ungodly." Fix your mind on that, and rest there.

Let this one great, gracious, glorious fact lie in your spirit till it perfumes all your thoughts, and makes you rejoice even though you are without strength, seeing the LORD Jesus has become your strength and your song. He has become your salvation. In the Scriptures it is a revealed fact that in due time Christ died for the ungodly when they were without strength.

Jesus did not die for our righteousness, but He died for our sins. He did not come to save us because we were worth the saving, but because we were utterly worthless, ruined, and undone.

He didn't come to earth for any reason that was in us, but solely and only out of reasons which He fetched from the depths of His own divine love. In due time He died for those whom He describes, not as godly, but as ungodly, applying to them as hopeless an adjective as He could well have selected. If you have slight understanding, fasten to this truth, which is fitted to the smallest capacity, and is able to cheer the heaviest heart.

Let this text lie under your tongue like a sweet candy, until it dissolves in your heart and flavors all your thoughts; and then it will matter little when your thoughts are as scattered as autumn leaves.

-CHARLES SPURGEON

Christ died for the very least of us. It matters not our skills or intelligence. He is the Shepherd who goes after the one lost sheep while the rest sit safely in their pen. Pray for help, and God will carry you where you need to go.

THE GIFT OF THE HOLY SPIRIT

[Jesus said,] "I am sending forth the promise
of My Father upon you; but you are to stay in the city until
you are clothed with power from on high."

LUKE 24:49 NASB

"The outpouring of the Holy Spirit is the crowning event of all the great events of salvation."

-ABRAHAM KUYPER

One of God's greatest gifts is the Holy Spirit dwelling inside believers, giving them comfort and power to live the life of love and faith that they never had before they met Jesus Christ. William Law (1686-1761) states it in no uncertain terms:

I would not turn my own thoughts, or call the attention of Christians, to anything but the one thing necessary, the one thing essential and the only thing available for our rising out of our fallen state and becoming, the way we were at our creation: a holy child of God, and a real partaker of the divine nature.

If you asked what this one thing is, it is the Spirit of God brought again to His first power of life in us [as in Adam]. Nothing else is needed by us; nothing else intended for us, but the Law, the prophets, and the Gospel. Nothing else is, or can be effectual, for making a sinful person become again a godly saint.

All Scripture bears full witness to this truth. The end and design of all that is written is only to call us back from the spirit of Satan, the flesh, and the world, to be again under full dependence upon, and obedience to the Spirit of God, who out of free love and thirst after our souls, seeks to have His first power of life in us.

When this is done, all is done that the Scripture can do for us. For if it be an unchangeable truth, that "no one can say that Jesus is LORD except by the Holy Spirit," it must be a truth equally unchangeable, that no one can have any single Christ-like temper or power of goodness except as he is immediately led and governed by the Holy Spirit (1 Corinthians 12:3 NKJV).

-WILLIAM LAW (CONDENSED FROM A LARGER PASSAGE)

Have you been frustrated by your lack of progress as a Christian? Look to God's provision of His Spirit and spend time with Him often. In time, God himself will bear the fruits of virtue that you long for in your life.

THE HOPE OF HEAVEN

We give thanks to God, the Father of our LORD Jesus Christ, praying always for you, because of the hope laid up for you in heaven, of which you previously heard in the word of truth.

COLOSSIANS 1:3,5 NASB

When our hope is in heaven, our whole outlook on life changes. We go from being frustrated and fearful when things go wrong, to cheerfully marching forward with a clear sight of victory. The evangelist Dwight L. Moody says we are to read our Bibles with great hope and expectation, for all the magnificent descriptions of heaven are there for our encouragement.

A great many people imagine that anything said about heaven is only a matter of speculation. They talk about heaven much as they would about the air. Now there would not have been so much in Scripture on this subject if God had wanted to leave the human race in darkness about it. "All Scripture," we are told, "is given by inspiration of God, and is profitable for doctrine, for reproof, for correction, for instruction in righteousness, that the man of God may be complete, thoroughly equipped for every good work" (2 Timothy 3:16-17 NKJV).

What the Bible says about heaven is just as true as what it says about everything else. The Bible is inspired. What we are taught about heaven could not have come to us in any other way than by divine inspiration. No one knew anything about it but

God, and so if we want to find out anything about it we have to turn to His word. Dr. Hodge, of Princeton, says that the best evidence of the Bible being the word of God is to be found between its own two covers. It proves itself. In this respect it is like Christ, whose character proclaimed the divinity of His person. Christ showed Himself as more than human by what He did. The Bible shows itself more than a human book by what it says.

-DWIGHT L. MOODY

Let us put our hope in the heaven of God's Word. The heaven in the Bible is more than playing harps and wearing white clothes; it is an unending, exciting time spent with the God and Creator of the universe. Let us use this hope as a new perspective on our daily lives that will give us courage and patience.

"The patience of hope does not turn men and women into monks and nuns, it gives men and women the right use of this world from another world's standpoint."

-OSWALD CHAMBERS

ABIDE IN HOPE

Christ in you, the hope of glory.

COLOSSIANS 1:27 NKJV

There are so many phrases in the Bible, so many names of God, that we tend to skim over them when we read. But these names, when we stop and consider them, are full of relevance and hope. Christ is indeed in us and our hope of glory.

The author Barbara Kingsolver said, "The very least you can do in your life is to figure out what you hope for. And the most you can do is live inside that hope. Not admire it from a distance but live right in it, under its roof." This is true of our love and our dreams. If we know ourselves and what we love and hope for, we can head in the right direction. We can also enjoy and grow while we follow our dreams because we are in the center of what we love.

But this is the same for our spiritual lives. If we live in our hope, we will flourish now and in the future. Our hope is Christ. He is "our living hope" and our "hope of glory" (1 Timothy 1:1 MSG; Colossians 1:27 NKJV).

If we only ask for Christ's hope so we can go to heaven rather than hell, we are missing out. We lose the true purpose of God's plan for His children, for us to live in joy and hope in the midst of evil and suffering in the world.

God, help me to live in You each day. Help me to seek You in the morning and before I go to bed. Remind me to drink from Your living Word in the Bible. Help me to see Your hand at work in my life and in the lives around me. And may my joy in Your presence grow more and more as I dwell in Christ, my living hope. I love and praise You, for You are full of love and compassion. Amen.

I look up—into the face of Jesus,
For there my heart can rest, my fears are stilled.
And there is joy, and love, and light for darkness,
And perfect peace, and every hope fulfilled.

-ANNIE JOHNSON FLINT

GRACE, LOVE,
AND MERCY

Where sin abounded, grace did much more abound.

ROMANS 5:20 KJV

God is naturally full of grace, love, and mercy for us. And when we are able to realize how great His love for us is, in the face of our own flaws and failures, we then can appreciate, accept, and shine in His redeeming grace. The writer of *Pilgrim's Progress*, John Bunyan, explains the different slant of the words *grace, love,* and *mercy* as we approach God in our weakness.

I find that the goodness of God to His people is expressed differently in His Word, sometimes by the word *grace,* sometimes by the word *love,* and sometimes by the word *mercy.*

When it is expressed by that word *grace,* then it is to show that what He does is of His princely will, His royal bounty, and sovereign pleasure.

When it is expressed by that word *love,* then it is to show us that His affection was and is in what He does, and that He does what He does for us with satisfaction and delight.

But when it is set forth to us under the notion of *mercy,* then it says that we are in a wretched and miserable state, and that His heart and compassion yearn over us in our fearful plight.

Some people say that when grace and a good personality meet together, they do make shining Christians. But I say, When grace

and a great sinner meet, and when grace shall subdue that great
sinner to itself, and shall work in the soul of that great sinner,
then we have a shining Christian.

-JOHN BUNYAN

God is indeed full of grace, love, and mercy. He is magnificent,
affectionate, and forgiving of all people; and He desires that they
turn to Him to accept the joyous gift of His presence and glory.

"God is none other than the Savior of our wretchedness. So
we can only know God well by knowing our iniquities. Those
who have known God without knowing their wretchedness have
not glorified Him, but have glorified themselves."

-BLAISE PASCAL

FREEDOM IN CHRIST

*[God] upholds the cause of the oppressed and gives food to the hungry.
The LORD sets prisoners free.*

PSALM 146:7 NIV

In many ways we should disagree with George MacDonald
(1824-1905) when he says that Christ didn't die to save us from
suffering or injustice. It seems a blasphemous remark when we
consider that Christ said He came "to proclaim freedom for the
prisoners and . . . to release the oppressed" (Luke 4:18 NIV). The
whole Sermon on the Mount and countless psalms argue that
God loves the humble and will take care of and rescue His people. However, when we read further, MacDonald's point seems to
be that God cares more about our spiritual oppression than our
physical suffering.

Christ died to save us, not from suffering, but from ourselves;
not from injustice, far less from justice, but from being unjust. He
died that we might live—but live as He lives, by dying as He
died—who died to Himself that He might live unto God. If we
do not die to ourselves, we cannot live to God, and He that does
not live to God, is dead. "And you shall know the truth," the LORD
says, "and the truth shall make you free" (John 8:32 NJKV).

Jesus has shown us the Father not only by doing what the
Father does, not only by loving His Father's children even as the
Father loves them, but by His perfect satisfaction with Him, His

joy in Him, His utter obedience to Him. He has shown us the Father by the absolute devotion of a perfect son. He is the Son of God because the Father and He are one, have one thought, one mind, one heart.

Upon this truth—I do not mean the doctrine, but the truth itself of Jesus to His Father—hangs the universe; and upon the recognition of this truth—that is, upon their becoming thus true—hangs the freedom of the children, the redemption of their whole world. "I and My Father are one," is the center—truth of the Universe; and the circling truth is, "that they also may be one in Us" (John 10:30; 17:21 NKJV).

The only free people, then, are those who are children of the Father. They are servants of all, but can be made the slaves of none. They are children of the LORD of the universe.

-GEORGE MACDONALD

Christian freedom comes from the unity between Christians and Christ, and Christ and God. And if we are one in Christ and with Christ, we can be free to act in love and peace to all who come across our path.

GOD'S GRACE TO
LIVE BY FAITH

*The grace of our LORD was poured out on me abundantly, along with
the faith and love that are in Christ Jesus.*

1 TIMOTHY 1:14 NIV

George Müller, in the early 1800s, felt led to live a life entirely
by faith and to record his experiences in a journal to share and
encourage others to do the same. He began as a preacher and
then opened up orphanages and day schools, which eventually
supported over 2,000 children. The whole time he refused to ask
anyone but God for money or support. And God blessed him, his
family, and his staff abundantly.

It wasn't always easy to wait on God's timing for provisions.
They never went without the essentials of food, clothing, or shelter, but often money or food would arrive in the mail or by hand
just minutes before it was needed. However, each year God
blessed Müller and his charities with more money than the year
before. The following excerpt from Müller's diary encourages
every Christian to depend on God for all of their needs.

By the grace of God I desire that my faith in God should
extend toward everything, the smallest of my own physical and
spiritual concerns, and the smallest of the physical and spiritual
concerns of my family, my co-workers, and my church members.

Do not think that I have achieved in faith as much as I could and ought to achieve; but thank God for the faith which He has given me, and ask Him to uphold and increase it.

Once more, let not Satan deceive you in making you think that you could not have the same faith, and that it is only for persons who are situated as I am. When I lose a small thing, such a thing as a key, I ask the LORD to direct me to it, and I look for an answer to my prayer. When a person I have an appointment with doesn't come on time, and I begin to be inconvenienced by it; I ask the LORD to be pleased to hurry them to me, and I look for an answer. When I do not understand a passage of God's Word, I lift up my heart to the LORD, that He would be pleased, by His Holy Spirit, to teach me. And I expect to be taught, although I do not set the time when and the manner how it should be explained. When I am going to minister the word, I seek help from the LORD. While I—conscious of my natural inability and utter unworthiness—begin His service, I am not cast down, but cheerful because I look for His assistance and believe that He, for His Son's sake, will help me.

And therefore, in all of my physical and spiritual concerns I pray to the LORD, and expect an answer to my requests. May you not do the same? Oh! I implore you, do not think me an extraordinary believer, having privileges above other of God's dear children, which they cannot have. Don't look on my way of acting as something that would not work for other believers. Make a test! Do but stand still in the hour of test, and you will see the help of God, if you trust in Him.

-GEORGE MÜLLER

You can depend on God for everything. He cares about your lost keys, your health, and your finances. Ask the LORD what area of your life He wants you to turn over to Him, and trust that He will abundantly provide and bless you.

"The LORD has blessed us abundantly."

JOSHUA 17:14 NIV

STRUGGLING WITH HOPELESSNESS

Why are you cast down, O my soul?
And why are you disquieted within me?
Hope in God; for I shall yet praise Him,
The help of my countenance and my God.

PSALM 42:11 NKJV

There are times in everyone's life when we feel depressed and without hope. Sometimes the cause is our circumstances. Our family is struggling, our friends need help, and our jobs stress us out. Other times, our situations are okay, but we are weary from the busyness of life. The following poem, "A Better Resurrection," by Christina Rossetti (1830-1894) is a cry to God similar to the psalms of David. It begins with descriptions of pain and emptiness but ends with a plea for God's saving grace.

I have no wit, no words, no tears;
My heart within me like a stone
Is numbed too much for hopes or fears.
Look right, look left, I dwell alone;
I lift mine eyes, but dimmed with grief
No everlasting hills I see;
My life is in the falling leaf:
O Jesus, quicken me.

My life is like a faded leaf,
My harvest dwindled to a husk:
Truly my life is void and brief
And tedious in the barren dusk;
My life is like a frozen thing,
No bud nor greenness can I see:
Yet rise it shall—the sap of spring;
O Jesus, rise in me.

My life is like a broken bowl,
A broken bowl that cannot hold
One drop of water for my soul
Or cordial in the searching cold;
Cast in the fire the perished thing;
Melt and remold it, till it be
A royal cup for Him, my King:
O Jesus, drink of me.

-CHRISTINA ROSSETTI

Oh, that we would be changed and made useful tools for God. Not to only help or save others, but to serve and please our LORD and King. May our praises be a sweet offering to the God who loves to bless us.

BY GRACE NOT MERIT

By grace you have been saved through faith;
and that not of yourselves, it is the gift of God.

EPHESIANS 2:8 NASB

There are many people who still believe that they will go to
heaven by "being good" and "doing good things." Some just try in a
general way to do more good than bad. Then there are those who
have lists of hard rules to obey to "be good" and to be a Christian.

But being a Christian is more than obeying rules or "being
good." It is centered on a continuing, personal relationship with
God. God's grace or gift to us is the forgiveness and canceling of
our sins, which keep us from reaching Him.

When Christ died on the cross, He was the ultimate sacrifice.
We didn't have to keep struggling and failing to earn our salvation. Martin Luther writes that before Christ, before the Israelites
even had the law of Moses, God counted Abraham and others
righteous because of their faith in His grace.

To reject the grace of God, is a horrible sin commonly reign-
ing throughout the world. All who seek righteousness by their
own works are guilty of this. For while they seek to be justified by
their own works and merits, or by the law, they reject the grace of
God and Christ.

If a rich man . . . should adopt a stranger, whom he owes
nothing, to be his son, and should then appoint him to be the

heir of all his lands and goods, and then years later he should set upon the son a law to do this or that; the son cannot then say that he has deserved this inheritance by his own works and obedience of this law.

For years the father asked nothing and the son had received the same inheritance freely and by his mere favor. It is the same with God, who could not respect our works and merits as granting our righteousness; for the promise and the gift of the Holy Spirit was four hundred and thirty years before the law.

Abraham did not obtain righteousness before God through the law. For there was no law yet. If there were no law yet, then there was neither work nor merit. What then? Nothing else but the mere promise of God. This promise Abraham believed, and it was counted to him as righteousness.

-MARTIN LUTHER

Christ died on the cross for our sins. He did this before we were born and before we could try to prove ourselves perfect and worthy of His grace. We don't have to be perfect on our own. We can accept His forgiveness and grace, and rest simply in His presence.

HOPE BASED ON FAITH

Let us fix our eyes on Jesus, the author and perfecter of our faith.

HEBREWS 12:2 NIV

Faith, hope, and love are difficult concepts to grasp. We can easily use them in a sentence, but when asked if we have them, it is hard to be sure. A better question would be, what do you have faith in, or hope in, or love? When the object of our faith is in focus, then our faith is a mere tool by which we understand and rely upon it. John Bunyan explains that hope relies on faith because faith relies upon God and His promises.

Without faith there is no hope. To hope without faith, is to see without eyes, or to expect without grounds; for "faith is the assurance of things hoped for" (Hebrews 11:1 NASB).

Faith will do what hope cannot do, hope can do what faith cannot do, and love can do things distinct from both of them. Faith goes in the front, hope in the middle, and love brings up the rear.

Faith is the mother-grace, for hope is born of her, but love flows from them both.

Faith comes by hearing, and hope by experience. Faith comes by hearing the Word of God, hope by the trust that faith has given to it. Faith believes the truth of the Word, hope waits for the fulfilling of it. Faith lays hold of that end of the promise that is next to us, but hope lays hold of that end of the promise that is fastened to the mercy-seat. For the promise is like a mighty cable that is fastened by one end to a ship, and by the other to the anchor. The soul is the ship where faith is, and to which the end of this cable is fastened; but hope is the anchor that is at the other end of this cable, and "which enters the Presence behind the veil" (Hebrews 6:19 NKJV).

-JOHN BUNYAN

If we are still confused by the amount of our faith and hope and whether they are strong enough for us to remain afloat, we are missing the point. All that is necessary for us as Christians is to focus on Christ who is our hope and in whom our faith rests.

A faith in nothing is no faith. We are only as strong as what we believe in. A faith in Christ is as strong as Christ. When we hope in Christ, the author of our faith, we will not be let down.

When darkness seems to hide His face,
I rest on His unchanging grace.
In every high and stormy gale,
My anchor holds within the veil.

-EDWARD MOTE

THE WILL AND HOPE

As for me, I will hope continually,
And will praise You yet more and more.

PSALM 71:14 NASB

Many times it is hard to continue to hold on to our hope in the face of troubling and painful circumstances. Our negative emotions often get the best of us. Instead of rejoicing in hope, we feel overcome by grief, depression, anger, worry, and fear. But Christian hope is not only an emotion; it is a strong determination to continue on with a firm grip on our faith in a good, saving God. Hannah Whitall Smith gives an example of submitting our emotions to our will and daily allowing hope to increase.

The will is like a wise mother in a nursery; the feelings are like a set of clamoring, crying children. The mother decides upon a certain course of action, which she believes to be right and best. The children yell against it, and declare it shall not be.

But the mother, knowing that she is the boss and not they, pursues her course calmly, unmoved by their noise, and takes no notice of them except in trying to soothe and quiet them. The result is that the children are sooner or later compelled to yield, and fall in with the decision of the mother. Therefore order and harmony are preserved.

But if that mother should for a moment let in the thought that the children were the boss instead of her, confusion would reign unchecked. Such instances have been known in family life!

And in how many souls at this very moment is there nothing but confusion, simply because the feelings are allowed to govern, instead of the will!

-HANNAH WHITALL SMITH

Usually emotions are echoes of thoughts and situations that we encounter each day. However, they can become confused or stuck in certain cycles. When we give too much credit to our emotions and trust them rather than analyzing where they come from, they can increase and echo louder than the original cause. When we listen to our emotions and decide they are exaggerated, we need to continue the course and they will eventually follow.

Many times we become discouraged or scared to continue. We sink in our feelings like quicksand and begin to drown. But when we cry to God for help, He will give us hope. He will be our life preserver that keeps us afloat and able to continue following Him.

RETURNING TO GRACE

[Jesus said,] "When he was still a long way off, his father saw him.
His heart pounding, he ran out, embraced him, and kissed him. . . .
'We're going to feast! We're going to have a wonderful time!
My son is here—given up for dead and now alive!
Given up for lost and now found!'"

LUKE 15:20,23-24 MSG

The famous songwriter William J. Kirkpatrick (1838-1921) was born in Pennsylvania in 1838. He wrote his first collection of hymns at twenty-one, and by his death at age eighty-three had written fifty books of music.

The words to the following song, "LORD, I'm Coming Home," were written for a specific purpose—to win the soul of the young soloist hired to sing it. Kirkpatrick had noticed that the soloist left each night before the sermon began. He prayed for the man to stay, hear the sermon, and to know the LORD. While he was praying, the words to a song came into his mind. He quickly jotted down the words and gave them to the soloist to sing.

I've wandered far away from God,
Now I'm coming home;
The paths of sin too long I've trod,
LORD, I'm coming home.

Coming home, coming home,
Nevermore to roam,
Open wide Thine arms of love,
LORD, I'm coming home.

I've wasted many precious years,
Now I'm coming home;
I now repent with bitter tears,
LORD, I'm coming home.

I'm tired of sin and straying, LORD,
Now I'm coming home;
I'll trust Thy love, believe Thy Word,
LORD, I'm coming home.

My soul is sick, my heart is sore,
Now I'm coming home;
My strength renew, my hope restore,
LORD, I'm coming home.

My only hope, my only plea,
Now I'm coming home;
That Jesus died, and died for me.
LORD, I'm coming home.

I need His cleansing blood, I know,
Now I'm coming home;
O wash me whiter than the snow,
LORD, I'm coming home.

At the end of the song, the soloist was visibly moved. He stayed for the sermon and then went forward to give his life to Christ. Kirkpatrick's song helped convince the young man of the relief and joy there is when one turns to Christ and accepts His compassionate grace.

HOPING AND
ASPIRING TO LOVE

Since we have confidence to enter the holy place by the blood of Jesus. . . .
let us draw near with a sincere heart in full assurance of faith,
having our hearts sprinkled clean from an evil conscience and
our bodies washed with pure water.

HEBREWS 10:19,22 NASB

If a child wants dinner, they place hope in their mother's ability to make it on time, but they move beyond hope to action by washing their hands and helping set the table. Frances de Sales (1567-1622) calls that kind of preparation "aspiration" and explains how this child is like us waiting on the love and help of God. We hope to have God's love as He promised. But we then take steps to receive that same love—we aspire. We have hope because we know and trust God to keep His promises. And we aspire by reaching out and accepting God's gift of grace and love, and then obeying Him.

And indeed, between hoping and aspiring there is but this difference, that we hope for those things which we expect to get by another's assistance, and we aspire unto those things which we think to reach by means that lie in our own power. And since we attain the fulfillment love, which is God, by His favor, grace and mercy. Yet the same mercy will have us co-operate with His favor, by adding the weakness of our consent to the strength of his grace. Our hope is then mingled with aspiring, so that we do not altogether hope without aspiring, nor do we ever aspire without entirely hoping.

Aspiration is a child of hope, as our co-operation is of grace; those that would hope without aspiring would be rejected as cowardly and negligent. And those that would aspire without hoping would be rash, insolent, and presumptuous. But when hope is followed with aspiration, and when, hoping we aspire and aspiring we hope, then hope by aspiration becomes a courageous desire, and aspiration is changed by hope into a humble claim, and we hope and aspire as God inspires us.

But both are caused by that desiring love, which tends to do us good—and the more surely it is hoped for, the more it is loved. Yes, hope is no other thing than the loving complacency we take in the expecting and seeking to be in God's presence. All that is there is love.

-FRANCES DE SALES

As we aspire to know God and spend time with Him, we can hope in His promise that He will speak to us and bless us.

THE SIXTH SENSE OF FAITH

We do not lose heart, but though our outer man is decaying, yet our inner man is being renewed day by day. We look not at the things which are seen, but at the things which are not seen; for the things which are seen are temporal, but the things which are not seen are eternal.

2 CORINTHIANS 4:16,18 NASB

A faith in God is not optimism if it is based on a reality that is stronger than the observed reality. There is a truth stronger than what is obvious. This is the truth that we catch glimpses of when reading the Bible. God's Word is full of explanations and promises to the children of God. That they believe these promises and act on them isn't as foolish as it seems to others, but wise. They rely on God for their happy ending. Oswald Chambers preached that faith is a sixth sense that gives Christians hope that increases when they read the Bible and act on it.

The faith of the saints is a God-given sixth sense which takes a hold of the spiritual facts that are revealed in the Bible. The hope of the Christian is the expectation and certainty of human nature transfigured by faith. Keep in mind that hope that is not transfigured by faith dies. Hope without faith loses itself in vague speculation, but the hope of the saints transfigured by faith doesn't grow faint, but endures "as seeing Him who is invisible" (Hebrews 11:27 NKJV).

-OSWALD CHAMBERS

If our hope is mere optimism, we will be disappointed, but if we hope in God and read the Scriptures to increase our faith, we will always have God's truth to depend on.

> *Jesus, I hang upon Thy Word;*
> *I steadfastly believe*
> *Thou wilt return and claim me, Lord,*
> *And to Thyself receive.*
>
> -CHARLES WESLEY

THE MIRACLE OF
GRACE IN A SOUL

You are not in the flesh but in the Spirit,
if indeed the Spirit of God dwells in you.

ROMANS 8:9 NASB

God touches our souls and gives us both the desire for Him and the ability to reach Him. The thirteenth-century Christian writer Meister Eckhart (1260-1328) says that God gives us grace to make us ready for the bigger gift of himself. With His gift of grace, we are able let Him dwell in us and work through us.

What God makes in the simple light of the soul is more beautiful and more delightful than all the other things He creates. Through that light comes grace.

Grace never comes in the intelligence or in the will. If it could come in the intelligence or in the will, the intelligence and the will would have to rise above themselves. The true union between God and the soul takes place in the little spark, which is called the spirit of the soul. Grace doesn't take any work to unite. It is an indwelling and a living together of the soul in God.

Every gift of God makes the soul ready to receive a new gift, greater than itself.

God has never given any gift, so people might rest in the possession of the gift, but gives every gift that He has given in heaven and on earth, in order that He might be able to give one main gift, which is himself. So with this gift of grace, and with all His gifts, He will make us ready for the one gift, which is himself.

No one is so coarse or stupid or awkward, that they cannot, by God's grace, unite their will wholly and entirely with God's will. And nothing more is necessary than that they should say with earnest longing: O Lord, show me Your dearest will, and strengthen me to do it.

And God does it, as sure as He lives, and gives them grace in ever richer fullness, until they come to perfection.

O almighty and merciful Creator and good LORD, be merciful to me for my poor sins, and help me that I may overcome all temptations and shameful desires, and may be able to avoid utterly, in thought and deed, what You forbid. And give me grace to do and to hold all that You have commanded. Help me to believe, to hope, and to love, and in every way to live as You will, as much as You will, and what You will. Amen.

-MEISTER ECKHART

THE ACTIVE POWER OF
GRACE AND HOPE

*We do not have the excuse of ignorance, everything—and I do mean
everything—connected with that old way of life has to go. It's rotten
through and through. Get rid of it! And then take on an entirely new
way of life—a God-fashioned life, a life renewed from the inside.*

While we are now saved by the gift of grace and not by our
works and obedience, this does not mean we can remain inactive
or continue in our old ways and habits. They are rotten and need
to be replaced. God's commandments were designed to let us
know just that. But now as Christians we have the power, or ability, to change.

The Christian life is based on a foundational abiding in
Christ. We abide more and more through prayer and reading
God's Word. This abiding produces and works through us many
good things. We then, naturally, change our old ways; we become
more loving and able to help others. The English Puritan, Richard
Baxter (1615-1691), writes of the natural tendency of God's grace
to propel us toward action.

Let us further consider that it is the nature of every grace to
promote diligence, that trifling in the way to heaven is lost labor,
that much precious time is already wasted, and that our reward

will be in proportion to our labor.

See the nature and tendency of every grace. If we loved God, we would think nothing too much that we could possibly do to serve Him and please Him. Love is quick and impatient, active and observant. If we loved Christ, we would keep His commandments, not accuse them of being too strict. If we had faith, it would quicken and encourage us.

If we had the hope of glory, it would, as the spring in the watch, set all the wheels of our souls moving. If we had the fear of God, it would rouse us out of inactivity. If we had zeal, it would inflame, and "eat us up." In what degree we are sanctified, in the same degree we will be serious and hardworking in the work of God.

-RICHARD BAXTER

O God, there are many times when we find it easier to float along without Your help, without changing or helping others. Give us the strength and desire to daily read the Bible and pray so we can know You and become more like You as You give us Your grace. Amen.

"Men may fall by sin, but cannot raise themselves up without the help of grace."

-JOHN BUNYAN

THE JOY OF HIS PRESENCE

[Jesus said,] "Behold, I stand at the door and knock; if anyone hears My voice and opens the door, I will come in to him and will dine with him, and he with Me."

REVELATION 3:20 NASB

Jesus welcomes us to enjoy the privilege of a vital and present-moment relationship of love with Him that goes beyond mere Bible reading and church attendance. He calls His children to spend time with Him and to expect real conversation to take place. William Law points to the role of the Holy Spirit in accomplishing the miracle of true friendship with God.

Again, Christ, after His glorification in heaven, says, "Behold, I stand at the door and knock." He does not say, "Behold, you have Me in the Scriptures."

Now what is the door at which Christ, at the right-hand of God in heaven, knocks? Surely it is the heart, to which Christ is always present.

He goes on, "if any one hears My voice." How do they hear but by the hearing of the heart, or what voice, but that which is the speaking or sounding of Christ within them? He adds, "and opens the door," that is, a living holy nature and spirit will be born within him, "and will dine with him, and he with Me." Behold the last finishing work of a redeeming Jesus, entered into the heart that opens to Him, bringing forth the joy, the blessing, and perfection of that first life of God in the soul, which was lost by the fall, set forth as a supper, or feast of the heavenly Jesus with the soul, and the soul with Him.

Now this continual knocking of Christ at the door of the heart, sets forth the case or nature of a continual immediate divine inspiration within us; it is always with us, but there must be an opening of the heart to it; and though it is always there, yet it is only felt and found by those who are attentive to it, depend upon, and humbly wait for it. Now let anyone tell me how they can believe anything of this voice of Christ, how they can listen to it, hear, or obey it, except by such a faith, as keeps them habitually turned to an immediate constant inspiration of the Spirit of Christ within them!

-WILLIAM LAW

Open your heart today and ask God to teach you how to hear His voice and be one of His friends.

JESUS' POWER
THROUGH YOU

"I have been crucified with Christ; and it is no longer I who live, but Christ lives in me; and the life which I now live in the flesh I live by faith in the Son of God, who loved me and gave Himself up for me."

GALATIANS 2:20 NASB

One of the most difficult things to grasp about the Christian life is that it is to be lived by God's power and not by the strength of human effort or human willpower. Watchman Nee (1903-1972) learned this by his own struggles and the subsequent realization that God must accomplish the Christian life within him. He concludes:

The operation of His life in us is in a true sense spontaneous, that is to say, it is without effort of ours. The all-important rule is not to "try" but to "trust," not to depend upon our own strength but upon His. For it is the flow of life which reveals what we truly are "in Christ." It is from the Fountain of life that the sweet water issues.

Too many of us are caught acting as Christians. The life of many Christians today is largely a pretence. They live a "spiritual life," talk a "spiritual" language, adopt "spiritual" attitudes, but they are doing the whole thing themselves. It is the effort involved that should reveal to them that something is wrong. They force themselves to refrain from doing this, from saying that, from eating the other, and how hard they find it all!

Have we discovered how good the LORD is? Then in us He is as good as that! Is His power great? Then in us it is not less great! Praise God, His life is as mighty as ever, and in the lives of those who dare to believe the Word of God the divine life will be manifest in a power not one whit less mighty than was manifest of old.

-WATCHMAN NEE

Are you tired from trying so hard to be a Christian? Could it be you are doing it all with your own strength and not His? Ask Him to take over and to live His life through you.

> *Jesus, I am resting, resting*
> *In the joy of what Thou art.*
> *I am finding out the greatness*
> *Of Thy loving heart.*
>
> *Here I gaze and gaze upon Thee*
> *As Thy beauty fills my soul,*
> *For by Thy transforming power,*
> *Thou hast made me whole.*

-JEAN SOPHIA PIGOTT

HOPE AND FAITH
IN SILENT PRAYER

*"I'm speechless, in awe—words fail me.
. . . I'm ready to shut up and listen."*

JOB 40:4-5 MSG

Normally when we pray, we focus our will by choosing a subject to present to God or to think about. We read Scripture and respond to it, we follow the Lord's Prayer with its guidelines of Adoration, Confession, Thanksgiving, and Supplication, or we share with God what is going on in our lives, our fears, our hopes, our dreams. All of these are somewhat structured methods of prayer.

But silent prayer is different. The basis of silent prayer is waiting on God, focusing our will and love upon Him, and enjoying just spending time in His presence. Usually it takes practice to enjoy silent prayer. We start with a structured prayer or with verses from the Bible, and when something hits us and causes us to pause in wonder and amazement at the love of God, then we stop and enjoy that sensation. Madam Guyon (1648-1717) reminds us of the faith and hope it takes to sit down in silence and wait upon God. She gives basic instruction, encouraging enough for the timid beginner.

First, as soon as the soul by faith places itself in the Presence of God, and becomes aware of itself before Him, it should remain like this for a little time in a profound and respectful silence.

If, at the beginning, in forming the act of faith, it feels some little pleasing sense of the Divine Presence; it should remain there without being troubled for a subject, and go no farther. It should carefully cherish this sense of God while it continues. As soon as it subsides, the will may be excited by a tender feeling of love. If at the first suggestion of this feeling, the soul finds itself put back in that sweet peace, let it remain there. The smothered fire must be gently fanned; but as soon as it is lit, we must cease that effort, in case we extinguish it by our continued activity.

I would warmly recommend it to all, never to finish prayer, without remaining some little time after in a respectful silence. It is also of the greatest importance for the soul to go to prayer with courage, and such a pure and disinterested love, as seeks nothing from God, but the ability to please Him, and to do His will: for a servant who works hard for a large reward, renders themselves unworthy of any reward.

-MADAM GUYON

God will lift up and bless those who seek Him for himself. And since God is the Maker of all, He is worth more than anything He could give.

You will seek the LORD your God,
and you will find Him if you seek Him
with all your heart and with all your soul.

DEUTERONOMY 4:29 NKJV

COVENANT OF GRACE

[God said,] "And I will make you a great nation, and I will bless you,
and make your name great; and so you shall be a blessing; and I will
bless those who bless you, and the one who curses you I will curse. And
in you all the families of the earth will be blessed."

GENESIS 12:2-3 NASB

God's covenant with Israel was a solemn contract that He
would be their God and they would be His people. He would
lead them, care for them, and multiply them, as they loved, wor-
shiped, and obeyed Him. The Israelites had problems with the
contract because they, like all people, at times failed to obey God
and dedicate themselves to Him. But God is gracious and compassionate, slow to anger, and rich in love. (See Psalm 103:8.)

But God had a greater covenant planned for them and for us.
He sent His only Son to earth to work a new contract. François
Fenelon (1651-1715) writes of the amazing power of this second
covenant, a covenant of grace. It was a gift from God to us.

The important difference between the first covenant, or the
covenant of works, which said to men, "Do this and live," and the
second covenant, or the covenant of grace, which says, "Believe and
live," is this: The first covenant did not lead people to anything
that was perfect. It showed people what was right and good; but it
failed to give them the power to do what the covenant required.

People understood what was right and good, but they also knew what was evil. In their love and practice of evil, they no longer had power of themselves to flee from it.

The new or Christian covenant of grace, not only prescribes and commands, but also gives the power to fulfill.

-FRANÇOIS FENELON

God requires us to be perfect, and He then gives us the ability to obtain perfection through the death of the perfect Christ, and the power of the Holy Spirit transforming us from the inside out. All we must do is accept His gift, and daily spend time in His presence learning how to be open and willing to the Holy Spirit's working in and through us.

THE HOPE OF ABRAHAM

Abraham, who, contrary to hope, in hope believed. . . . He did not waver
at the promise of God through unbelief, but was strengthened in faith,
giving glory to God, and being fully convinced that what He had prom-
ised He was also able to perform. And therefore "it was accounted to him
for righteousness."

ROMANS 4:16,18,20-22 NKJV

Abraham had hope and believed God's promises to make his
descendents greater than the stars. This was a strong, amazing
hope. He and his wife were old and childless. This was before the
law, which God gave Moses, and even before the covenant
between God and Abraham with the outward sign of circumci-
sion. By following God and hoping, God counted him righteous.

Abraham didn't live perfectly after he heard from and followed God. He made many mistakes. He took Lot with him
when God said to leave all his family. (See Genesis 12:1,4.) He
lied in Egypt and said his wife was his sister. He slept with his
wife's maid, Hagar, instead of waiting for God to give him a child
through Sarah. (See Genesis 16:3-4.) But in spite of these mistakes, God counted him righteous. He was the patriarch of Israel,
the father of many nations. Scripture refers to him as God's servant and God's friend.

What does this mean for us? For God to consider us righteous, what do we need to do? The only thing necessary is God's

grace and our acceptance of it. Contrary to hope, we need to believe in hope. George Offor said, "Christian hope is a firm expectation of all promised good." The promises of the Bible are many and amazing. When we read, believe, and act on them in hope, our lives are meaningful and God blesses us over and over as we follow Him.

"Faith is an act. Faith is a leap. Faith jumps in. Faith claims. Faith's author is Jesus. He is the author and finisher of faith."

—SMITH WIGGLESWORTH

HOPE IN THE HOLY SPIRIT'S LEADING

[Jesus said,] "When He, the Spirit of truth, has come,
He will guide you into all truth."

JOHN 16:13 NKJV

We are often as individuals encouraged to wait on God for direction, but as groups we tend to use tradition, intelligence, and voting to get things done. Andrew Murray implores us that we are missing out on God's awesome plans and blessings when we don't seek His will first.

In our church worship, in our prayer meetings, in our conventions, in all our gatherings as managers or directors or committees or helpers in any part of the work for God, our first job must always be to be sure we understand the mind of God. God always works according to the counsel of His will. The more that counsel of His will is sought and found and honored, the more surely and mightily God will do His work for us and through us.

The great danger in all such groups is that in our consciousness of having our Bible, in our past experience of God's leading, in our sound creed and our honest wish to do God's will, we will trust in these and not realize that with every step we need and may have a heavenly guide. There may be elements of God's will, application of God's Word, experience of the close presence and leading of God, manifestations of the power of His Spirit, of which we know nothing as yet. God may be willing, no, God is willing to open up these in the souls who are intently set upon allowing Him to have His way entirely, and who are willing, in patience, to wait for Him to make it known.

When we come together praising God for all He has done and taught and given, we may, at the same time, be limiting Him by not expecting greater things. It was when God had given the water out of the rock that they did not trust Him for bread. It was when God had given Jericho into his hands that Joshua thought the victory over Ai was sure, and did not wait for counsel from God. And so, while we think that we know and trust the power of God for what we may expect, we may be hindering Him by not giving Him time, and not cultivating the habit of waiting for His counsel.

-ANDREW MURRAY

God, You are beyond our understanding. Your power is mighty. Your gifts are abundant. And Your plans are beyond our imagination. Increase our hope and trust in You. Let us learn to expect the unexpected! Amen.

Cornelius said [to Peter], "We are all present before God, to hear all the things commanded you by God."

ACTS 10:30,33 NKJV

A HOPE BEYOND
LIFE AND PAIN

Through thick and thin, keep your hearts at attention,
in adoration before Christ, your Master. Be ready to speak up and
tell anyone who asks why you're living the way you are,
and always with the utmost courtesy.

1 PETER 3:15 MSG

A young Civil War drummer, Charlie Coulson, placed his hope entirely in Jesus. Wounded, he refused chloroform or brandy because he had vowed not to ingest stimulants. The Jewish doctor proceeded to amputate brave Charlie's arm and leg. He never cried out and only prayed, "O Jesus, blessed Jesus! Stand by me now."

And Jesus did, but infection set in soon afterwards. His troubled doctor wrote:

Five days after, he sent for me. "Doctor," he said, "my time has come. Before I die I desire to thank you with all my heart for your kindness to me. Doctor, you are a Jew, you do not believe in Jesus; will you please stand here and see me die, trusting my Savior to the last moment of my life?"

I tried to stay, but I could not; for I had not the courage to stand by and see a Christian boy die rejoicing in the love of a Jesus whom I had been taught to hate.

About twenty minutes later a steward, who found me covering my face with my hand, said, "Doctor, Charlie Coulson wishes to see you."

I answered, "I cannot see him again."

"Doctor, he says he must see you once more before he dies."

When I reentered the hospital, I saw he was sinking fast. He said, "Doctor, I love you because you are a Jew; the best friend I have found in this world was a Jew."

I asked him who that was.

He answered, "Jesus Christ, to whom I want to introduce you before I die; and will you promise me, doctor, that what I am about to say to you, you will never forget?" I promised.

And he said, "While you amputated my arm and leg, I prayed to the LORD Jesus Christ to convert your soul."

These words went deep into my heart. I could not understand how, when I was causing him the most intense pain, he could forget all about himself and think of nothing but his Savior and my unconverted soul.

I would have given every penny I possessed if I could have felt towards Christ as Charlie did; but that feeling cannot be bought with money. I could not forget the boy. I now know that at that time I was under deep conviction of sin; but I fought against Christ for nearly ten years, until, finally, the dear boy's prayer was answered, and God converted my soul.

-DR. M.L.R. [TEXT CONDENSED]

Jesus, lover of my soul,
Let me to Thy bosom fly,
While the nearer waters roll,
While the tempest still is high.
Hide me, O my Savior, hide,
Till the storm of life is past;
Safe into the haven guide;
O receive my soul at last.

-CHARLES WESLEY

THE HOLY SPIRIT AND GRACE

*The Spirit himself testifies with our spirit that
we are God's children.*

ROMANS 8:16 NIV

Grace is a general term for the love and gifts that God gives us through His Spirit. Martin Luther writes of the Holy Spirit's power for grace and for prayer.

The Holy Spirit has two jobs. First, He is a Spirit of grace. He makes God gracious to us and receive us, for Christ's sake, as His acceptable children. Secondly, He is a Spirit of prayer. He prays for us, and for the whole world, so that all evil may be turned from us, and that all good may happen to us.

The spirit of grace teaches people. The spirit of prayer prays. It is a wonder how one thing is accomplished various ways. It is one thing to have the Holy Spirit as a spirit of prophecy, and another to have the revealing of the same; for many have had the Holy Spirit before the birth of Christ, and yet He was not revealed unto them.

-MARTIN LUTHER

God's grace is not only for our personal lives, but the Holy Spirit also gives us grace and prayer for others. When we live in the Spirit, we will flow with grace and forgiveness to those around us. We will have the words necessary to pray and explain to others the love of Christ. When we don't know what to pray for, the Holy Spirit will prompt us.

> *The Spirit helps us in our weakness.*
> *We do not know what we ought to pray for,*
> *but the Spirit himself intercedes for us with groans*
> *that words cannot express.*

ROMANS 8:26 NIV

GOD'S GRACE
REACHES ALL TYPES

[Jesus] said: "You're blessed when you're at the end of your rope. With less of you there is more of God and his rule. You're blessed when you feel you've lost what is most dear to you. Only then can you be embraced by the One most dear to you. You're blessed when you're content with just who you are—no more, no less. That's the moment you find yourselves proud owners of everything that can't be bought."

MATTHEW 5:2-5 MSG

When we are serving God, we will meet other servants of His. These random meetings aren't coincidences. God uses different members of the Body to encourage and build up each other in faith and joy. Catherine Marsh (1818-1912) writes in the pamphlet, *A Sketch of the Life of Captain Hedley Vicars*, of poor, starving men who continue to praise God for His blessing and goodness.

I was struck with proof that God is no respecter of persons, and has His own people in every class of people. I saw two wretched looking men picking up pieces of what I thought were rags in front of the guard tent. After they had collected several, they sat down.

I went to them, and found they were collecting pieces of meat and biscuit that had been thrown away by the men after dinner. These they ate ravenously. I got them some clean meat and talked with them for about ten minutes. They seemed surprised that an officer "in such fine clothes," talked to them about Christ. One of them had been a stoker in a railway, who had been run over by a train which had smashed his hand and foot, yet he could talk with delight of the mercy of God his Savior, and of His goodness and forbearance! Who knows but that I may meet and recognize these poor fellows in Heaven.

-CATHERINE MARSH

God, let us pay attention to those around us at the grocery store, in line at the bank, and on the street. Give us Your words to say and let us take part in Your compassion. Let us notice and help those who cross our path. Amen.

"You may call God love, you may call God goodness. But the best name for God is compassion."

-MEISTER ECKHART

HOPE PURIFIES

We know that when He appears,
we will be like Him, because we will see Him just as He is.
And everyone who has this hope fixed on Him purifies himself,
just as He is pure.

1 JOHN 3:2-3 NASB

Hope in Christ and heaven purifies us. It purifies us because we can go beyond our disappointments on earth. It purifies us because we can go beyond our sinful selves. We can depend on God instead of people. We can give up our anxieties and troubles because we know God will bless us through them. And we can be free to obey and take risks because even if we make mistakes, God won't abandon us but will, instead, seek us out in the darkest pit we end up in. George Offor (1787-1864) writes how the foundational hope in Christ purifies us.

Christian hope is a firm expectation of all promised good, but especially of eternal salvation and happiness in heaven, where we shall be like the Son of God. This hope is founded on the grace, blood, righteousness, and intercession of Christ—the earnest of the Holy Spirit in our hearts, and the unchangeable truths and enlightening power of God. "And everyone who has this hope fixed on Him purifies himself, just as He is pure" (1 John 3:3 NASB).

-GEORGE OFFOR

As Meister Eckhart writes, "Do exactly what you would do if you felt most secure." When we feel secure in our hope in God—that He loves us and continues to change us to be more like Him with His grace and love—then we will have the courage to make difficult decisions and really live for God. We can be brave and take leaps of faith because God's hope purifies and energizes us day by day.

DISOBEDIENCE
SHUTS OUT GRACE

*[Jesus said,] "He who does not take his cross and follow after Me is
not worthy of Me. He who finds his life will lose it, and he who loses
his life for My sake will find it."*

MATTHEW 10:38-39 NKJV

How can we call Jesus LORD and then not obey Him or follow Him completely? Catherine Booth (1829-1890), the
cofounder of the Salvation Army, writes about a young woman
who keeps trying to be "saved" but then cannot because she won't
obey Christ.

This lady said to me, almost passionately, "I believe the whole
of the New Testament—all about Jesus Christ, and I believe, that
He died for me, and that He makes intercession for me—and yet
I'm not saved a bit. I have no more power over sin than other people, and I know I am not saved. Now, what can be the reason? I
am afraid it is lack of faith."

"I do indeed want to be saved," she said. "I often go into my
room, and weep, and struggle, and pray for hours. I try to believe.
I think I have believed, and I come out and I am no better."

"Tell me, in these times when you say you go into your room,
and struggle, and pray, and strive, and believe; tell me, is there anything that comes up before the eye of your soul as an obstacle and

difficulty that has to be put away or embraced; anything that comes up and that the Spirit of God says, 'You must sacrifice this, or cut off that, or do something?' Just tell me that."

She was quiet for a moment and speechless. She waited; then she drew her breath and said, "Well, yes, I am afraid there is."

"Ah!" I said, "That is it. It is not lack of faith, it is lack of obedience. Now you may go on another ten years, going into your room, struggling and striving, but until you trample that under your feet, and say, 'LORD, I will follow You at all costs,' you won't be able to believe. . . . After experience with dealing with hundreds of souls just at this point, I tell you: you must give up that idol or embrace that cross, whatever it may be."

"Then," she said, "I will make no secret of it. I am the only member of an unconverted family that has no desire after God. My husband is a worldly, unconverted man, and I am in a worldly, unconverted circle. Always when I come to the LORD Jesus, it comes up before me that I will have to confess Him and to live like a Christian; and I am not willing to do so."

"Then, my dear lady, it is the old story over again of the Young Ruler. There you are; make your choice. You cannot be a Christian, and not confess Christ. You cannot be a Christian, and not live like one before your unconverted relatives. Therefore, if you are not willing to take up the cross and follow Him, you cannot become His disciple."

Then I went down on my knees with her, and we talked and prayed, and, at last, she said, "By the grace of God, I will confess Him."

Bless the LORD! The light of salvation soon appeared in her

eye, for it shone through her face. She found herself able to believe at once, and this is just the condition of thousands of souls. She got assurance then. She got saved. Before, she had been trying to believe she was saved, when she was not—quite a different thing to getting saved and then knowing it.

-CATHERINE BOOTH

If there is something holding you back from being saved or getting closer to Christ—give it up! It's not worth it compared to the joy and delight and peace you will find when you are able to be truly one with Christ!

THE GIFT OF FAITH

There are varieties of gifts, but the same Spirit. And there are varieties of ministries, and the same LORD. For to one is given the word of wisdom through the Spirit, and to another the word of knowledge according to the same Spirit; to another faith by the same Spirit.

1 CORINTHIANS 12:4-5, 8-9 NASB

Many realize that they need faith first, before they can believe, before they can have effective prayer, and before they can be healed or changed by God. However, most people consider this to be a difficult or tricky thing to do. They worry and try to work up enough faith for living a Christian life.

But faith is not something we have to worry about. Or at least, not in the way we think we do. Faith is a gift from God. It comes from above.

God gives us the faith to believe and to turn to Christ when we are still living in sin. And we can choose to act on this faith and follow Him, or we can choose to follow our own desires without Him.

Any further faith is also from God. The faith to continue believing, to conquer sin, and to heal is also from God. Faith is listed in 1 Corinthians 12 with the rest of the spiritual gifts that come from the Holy Spirit.

And if you are thinking, *Well, but I don't have very much of that gift,* you still don't have to worry. A little faith is very potent. Jesus tells those with little faith that all they need is the faith of a mustard seed to move a mountain.

The point of faith is not the faith itself, but the focus of that faith. If we have the tiniest drop of faith, and we put that faith in our God, who died on the cross and rose again, then He will do the rest.

[Jesus] said, . . . "Truly I say to you, if you have faith the size of a mustard seed, you will say to this mountain, 'Move from here to there,' and it will move; and nothing will be impossible to you."

MATTHEW 17:20 NASB

LORD, sometimes we are confused and lost. We worry that we can't make it, that we don't have enough faith to keep going. Thank You for our faith in You that gives us the strength, endurance, and hope to trust in Your promises, Your love, Your power, and Your good will. Amen.

GOD'S GRACE FOR BACKSLIDERS

"My people [says God] are bent on backsliding from Me."

HOSEA 11:7 NKJV

If we ever had to be good and win our salvation ourselves, we wouldn't even get close. We'd be doomed. We don't have the power or the purity to be good, to be holy, or to be worthy of the glorious God that is our Creator and Father.

Sometimes church-going Christians have trouble grasping how strong and wide God's grace truly is. We think that it is only the sinners, the former murderers, alcoholics, and overall bad people who can experience God's forgiving grace. But if we think about how many times we have slipped, how often we forget about God, how often we yell at our friends, how we ignore the poor and helpless, and how we tend to distort the truth and try to look good in all situations; then we realize that our little sins against God really add up. And still He continues to keep pardoning us. John Bunyan marvels at the grace of God to us as backsliders.

Suppose God doesn't discourage backsliding with negative consequences and discipline, but shines upon us again, and seals up to us the remission of our sins another time, saying, "I will heal their backsliding, I will love them freely" (Hosea 14:4 NKJV).

What will our soul do now? Surely it will walk humbly now, and holily all its days. It probably won't ever backslide again, will it?

Here is grace. So many times as the soul backslides, so many times God brings it back again—I mean the soul that must be saved by grace; He renews His pardons and multiplies them. For I know, there are some saints—and they not long-lived either— that must receive, before they enter into life, millions of pardons from God. Every pardon is an act of grace, through the redemption that is in Christ's blood.

The first step to the cure of a wounded conscience is for you to know the grace of God, especially the grace of God as to justification.

-JOHN BUNYAN

God's grace is all-encompassing of our sins and bad habits. It wraps around us and gives us new life. God longs to make us new creations as His beloved children.

I'll call nobodies and make them somebodies; I'll call the unloved and make them beloved. In the place where they yelled out, "You're nobody!" they're calling you "God's living children."

ROMANS 9:25-26 MSG

AVOIDING FALSE HOPE AND PRIDE

Trust in the LORD with all your heart,
And lean not on your own understanding;
In all your ways acknowledge Him,
And He shall direct your paths.

PROVERBS 3:5-6 NKJV

The treasures of this world are not our ultimate treasures. They are but examples or copies to show us the glories of heaven and the wonders of God. And our natural talents and abilities also come from God. They are just glimpses of what we can do in the future when we are submitted to God's will and used as a holy pipeline for His power. Thomas á Kempis (1379-1471) warns us that the treasures on earth are a false hope. They are empty and will lead to our emptiness and unhappiness. It is only God and His blessings that satisfy.

Those who place their trust in other people or in created things are foolish.

We should not be ashamed to serve others for the love of Jesus Christ and to seem poor in this world. Do not be self-sufficient but place your trust in God. Do what lies in your power, and God will aid your good will.

Put no trust in your own learning nor in the wisdom of anyone else, but rather put your trust in the grace of God—for He helps the humble and humbles the proud. If you have wealth, don't gloat about it. Also don't glory in your friends because they are powerful, but instead glory in God. God gives all things and desires above all to give Himself.

Do not boast of personal strength or of physical beauty, qualities which are marred and destroyed by a little sickness. Do not take pride in your talent or ability, in case you will displease God Who gave you all the natural gifts that you have.

Do not think yourself better than others because you might be judged worse before God, Who knows what is in a person. Do not take pride in your good deeds, for God's judgments differ from those of people; and what pleases them often displeases Him.

If there is good in you, see more good in others, so that you may remain humble. It does no harm to value yourself less than anyone else, but it is very harmful to think yourself better than even one. The humble live in continuous peace, while in the hearts of the proud are envy and frequent anger.

-THOMAS Á KEMPIS

THE UNSEEN VASTNESS OF GRACE

Where sin abounded, grace abounded much more.

ROMANS 5:20 NKJV

Grace is a term to describe the gratuitous love of God to people. This love is greater than our love, greater than any love, because God is perfect and enormous. He loves and cares for us, His created people. This grace that we talk about glides on our tongues without our thinking about it. But it is greater than what we can know or comprehend.

Grace is the tip of the iceberg. What we see is just the beginning of God, of His love and His plans for us. There is so much more—more love, more amazing plans, more of God, more of a blessed eternity with Him. (See Romans 8:32.) Hannah Whitall Smith encourages us to go beyond the human expectation of "much less" and depend on the biblical promise of "much more."

"Much less" is the language of the seen thing, "much more" is the language of the unseen thing. "Much less" seems on the surface to be far more reasonable than "much more," because every seen thing confirms it. Our weakness and foolishness are visible; God's strength and wisdom are invisible. Our need is obvious before our very eyes; God's supply is hidden in the secret of His presence, and can only be realized by faith.

It seems a paradox to tell us that we must see unseen things. How can it be possible? But there are other things to see than those which appear on surfaces, and other eyes to look through than those we generally use. An ox and a scientist may both look at the same field, but they will see very different things there.

To see unseen things requires us to have that interior eye opened in our souls which is able to see below surfaces, and which can pierce through the outer appearance of things into their inner realities. This interior eye looks not at the seen things, which are temporal, but at the things that are not seen, which are eternal; and the vital question for each one of us is, whether that interior eye has been opened in us yet, and whether we can see the things that are eternal, or whether our vision is limited to the things that are temporal only.

-HANNAH WHITALL SMITH

Open our eyes, LORD. We want to see You. We want to live beyond our expectations and depend on Your provision, Your plans, and Your love to satisfy us. Just as You have taught us to trust You more and more, let us trust You infinitely and turn in joyful obedience to do what You ask. Amen.

> *"You cannot trust God too much,*
> *nor trust yourself too little."*
>
> -CHARLES SPURGEON

THE HOPE OF
PERSEVERING PRAYER

[Nehemiah] said, "GOD, God-of-Heaven, the great and awesome God,
loyal to his covenant and faithful to those who love him and obey his
commands: Look at me, listen to me. Pay attention to this prayer of your
servant that I'm praying day and night in intercession for your servants."

NEHEMIAH 1:5-6 MSG

Prayer is the ability to hope in God and in His power and grace to change things. When our hearts are attuned to God, we pray, and miracles happen. The following story by C. H. Fowler shows a remarkable change made when God heard one man's prayer.

We knew a preacher who was appointed to the charge of a church in Springfield, Illinois. The church seemed very much depressed. Its life was fading. It was in the midst of the harvest, in the hot weather, when things seemed most depressed. The pastor, a holy man of God, announced on Sabbath evening to a small congregation of under fifty people, "There will be a prayer meeting in this church tomorrow morning at sunrise for the revival of the work of God and for the conversion of sinners." The people wondered at the notice, and went home.

The pastor went up into his study by the side of the church, and he gave that night to prayer. Just as the East began to lighten up a little with the coming day he had the assurance that his prayer was answered, and he lay down on a sofa for a little rest. Presently he awoke suddenly to see the sun shining on the wall over his head. He sprang up and looked out the window to see how late it was, and saw the sun just rising above the horizon.

Looking down into the yard by the church, he was overjoyed to see the church crowded with people, and the yard full, and teams crowding into the street for a long distance. God had heard his prayer, and had sent out His Spirit into the community, and there had been no sleeping in Springfield that night. People in the country who knew nothing of the meeting got up in the night, hitched up their teams, and drove into town and to the church to find out what the matter was. A good man had taken hold of God.

The prayer meeting began, and was closed that night at eleven o'clock. Several souls were converted. A gracious work broke out, and the community was greatly blessed.

-C. H. FOWLER

When we feel a burden for someone or even for a community or for the world, we should act on that feeling. Instead of getting disappointed or discouraged, we can turn our anguished feelings over to God in prayer and then join in the battle with God against sin and suffering and for the triumphant freedom of souls.

"When I pray, coincidences happen,
and when I do not, they don't."

-WILLIAM TEMPLE

RESISTING GOD
STOPS GRACE

*I keep Your precepts and Your testimonies, for all my ways are
before You. Let my cry come before You, O LORD;
Give me understanding according to Your word. Let my supplication
come before You; Deliver me according to Your word.*

PSALM 119:168-170 NKJV

The instant we stop and say, "But, I can't do that!" when God
makes a request or a demand, we freeze and miss out on both the
blessing of our obedience and the blessing of His presence.
Obedience is necessary for God's grace to flow freely to us.
Resisting God displays our active pride in ourselves and our fear
or unbelief of God's mercy and love. We can only accept what we
believe in, so when there is a stop in our soul and we turn our
back on God, we instantly miss out on God's love and grace.
François Fenelon emphatically reminds us to never doubt in God
and His love and ability to carry us through to follow His will.

You perceive, by the light of God, in the depth of your conscience, what grace demands of you, but you resist Him. This is
the cause of your distress. You begin to say within, it is impossible
for me to begin to do what is required of me.

This is a temptation to despair. Despair as much as you please
of yourself, but never despair of God. He is all good and all pow-

126

erful, and will grant you much according to your faith. If you will believe all things, all things shall be yours, and you shall remove mountains. If you believe nothing, you shall have nothing, but you alone will be to blame. Look at Mary, who, when the most incredible thing in the world was proposed to her, did not hesitate, but exclaimed; "may it be done to me according to your word" (Luke 1:38 NASB).

Open your heart then. It is now so shut up, that you not only don't have the power to do what is required of you, but you don't even desire to have it. You have no wish that your heart should be enlarged, and you fear that it will be. How can grace find room in so stiff a heart?

All that I ask of you is that you will rest in a teachable spirit of faith, and that you will not listen to yourself. Simply agree to everything with a submissive mind, and receive peace through recollection. Then everything will be gradually accomplished for you. Those things which in your hour of temptation and despair seemed the greatest difficulties will be insensibly smoothed away.

-FRANÇOIS FENELON

When Fenelon says God will grant you much according to your faith, he doesn't mean according to the feeling or amount of belief you have in Him. Faith is the active hope that turns to God and either waits for His promise to come true or takes the first step in obedience that He asks, knowing that God will handle the rest.

So once again, we can doubt in ourselves, but we can have great security and hope in the good and perfect nature of God.

SAVED BY GRACE

*It is by free grace (God's unmerited favor) that you are saved (delivered
from judgment and made partakers of Christ's salvation) through [your]
faith. And this [salvation] is not of yourselves [of your own doing, it
came not through your own striving], but it is the gift of God.*

EPHESIANS 2:8 AMP

Just as God didn't choose the Israelites because they were
important or worthy, He doesn't save us because of our abilities
or actions. Instead, our relationship with Him and our power
over sin comes directly as a free gift from God. Charles Spurgeon
compares God's gift of grace to a flowing fountain or a river full of
blessings.

Because God is gracious, therefore sinful men are forgiven,
converted, purified, and saved. It is not because of anything in
them, or that ever can be in them, that they are saved; but because
of the endless love, goodness, pity, compassion, mercy, and grace of
God. Wait a moment, then, at the fountain-head. Behold the pure
river of water of life, as it proceeds out of the throne of God and
of the Lamb!

What an abyss is the grace of God! Who can measure its
width? Who can grasp its depth? Like all the rest of the divine
attributes, it is infinite. God is full of love, for "God is love" (1
John 4:8 KJV). God is full of goodness; the very name "God" is
short for "good." Abundant goodness and love enter into the very

essence of the Godhead.

It is because "His mercy endures forever" that men are not destroyed; because "His compassions fail not" that sinners are brought to Him and forgiven (Psalm 136:1; Lamentations 3:22 NKJV).

-CHARLES SPURGEON

O God, I keep falling into sin, and Satan's lies tell me, "You can never be holy now." But I know that Your grace embraced me when I was still ignorant of You. I give to You my failures and rest in Your mercy and grace. Amen.

"The overflowing grace of God has no limits, and we have no set limits to it, but 'grow in grace, and in the knowledge of our LORD and Savior Jesus Christ.'"

-OSWALD CHAMBERS

THE LOVE OF GOD

As the deer pants for streams of water, so I long for you, O God.

PSALM 42:1 NLT

Even the desire to desire God comes from Him. His grace gives us the ability to know and enjoy His presence. A. W. Tozer (1897-1963) shares the writings of Frederick Faber to show the depth and passion of his love for God.

The highest love of God is not intellectual, it is spiritual. God is spirit and only the spirit of a person can know Him really. In the deep spirit of a person the fire must glow or their love is not the true love of God. The great of the Kingdom have been those who loved God more than others did. We all know who they have been and gladly pay tribute to the depths and sincerity of their devotion.

Fredrick Faber was one whose soul panted after God as the deer pants for the water. The amount God revealed Himself to Faber's seeking heart set his whole life afire with a burning adoration rivaling that of the seraphim before the throne. His love for God extended to the three Persons of the Godhead equally, yet he seemed to feel for each One a special kind of love reserved for Him alone. Of God the Father he sings:

> *Only to sit and think of God,*
> *Oh what a joy it is!*

To think the thought, to breathe the Name;
Earth has no higher bliss.

Faber's love for the Person of Christ was so intense that it
threatened to consume him; it burned within him as a sweet and
holy madness and flowed from his lips like molten gold. In one of
his sermons he says:

"Wherever we turn in the church of God, there is Jesus. He is
the beginning, middle and end of everything to us. There is nothing good, nothing holy, nothing beautiful, nothing joyous that He
is not to His servants. No one need be poor, because, if they
choose, they can have Jesus for their own property and possession.
No one need be depressed, for Jesus is the joy of heaven, and it is
His joy to enter into sorrowful hearts.

"We can exaggerate many things; but we can never exaggerate
our obligation to Jesus, or the compassionate abundance of the
love of Jesus to us. All our lives long we might talk of Jesus, and
yet we should never come to an end of the sweet things that
might be said of Him. Eternity will not be long enough to learn
all He is, or to praise Him for all He has done, but then, that
matters not; for we shall be always with Him, and we desire nothing more."

Addressing our LORD Christ directly, Faber says to Him:

I love Thee so, I know not how
My transports to control;
Thy love is like a burning fire
Within my very soul.

Faber's blazing love extended also to the Holy Spirit. Not only in his theology did he acknowledge His deity and full equality with the Father and the Son, but he celebrated it constantly in his songs and in his prayers. He literally pressed his forehead to the ground in his eager fervid worship of the Third Person of the Godhead. In one of his great hymns to the Holy Spirit he sums up his burning devotion with this:

> O Spirit, beautiful and dread!
> My heart is fit to break
> With love of all Thy tenderness
> For us poor sinners' sake.

God is so vastly wonderful, so utterly and completely delightful that He can, without anything other than Himself, meet and overflow the deepest demands of our total nature. Such worship as Faber knew can never come from a mere doctrinal knowledge of God.

-A. W. TOZER

God, give us a desire and a love of You as strong as Your love for us. Let us experience You in our daily lives so that everything else pales in comparison. Give us a deep passion to know You more and praise You constantly. Amen.

> "Real prayer comes not from gritting our teeth
> but from falling in love."

-RICHARD FOSTER

HOPE IN GOD ALONE

Find rest, O my soul, in God alone; my hope comes from him.

PSALM 62:5 NIV

Where can we find true happiness or joy? Who can understand and fulfill us more than anyone else? It is only in the presence of God that we can be satisfied and complete. Thomas á Kempis offers this prayer to remind us that we can only be happy when we put our hope in God, because God is the only One who will come through for us.

LORD, where is my trust in this life, or what is my greatest comfort among all the things under heaven? Is it not in You, O LORD, my God? Your mercies are without number. When have I ever fared well without You? How could things go badly when You were there?

I had rather be poor for Your sake than rich without You. I prefer rather to wander on the earth with You than to possess heaven without You. Where You are there is heaven, and death and hell are where You are not.

You are my desire, and therefore I must cry after You and sigh and pray. In none can I fully trust to help me in my needs, but in You alone, my God. You are my hope. You are my confidence. You are my comforter, most faithful in every need.

All people seek their own interests. You, however, place my salvation and my profit first, and turn all things to my good. Even when You expose me to various temptations and hardships, You, Who prove Your loved ones in a thousand ways, arrange all this for my good. You ought not to be loved or praised less in this bad situation than if You had filled me with heavenly blessings and comfort.

In You, therefore, O LORD God, I place all my hope and my shelter. On You I cast all my troubles and anguish, because whatever I have outside of You, I find to be weak and unstable.

-THOMAS Á KEMPIS

Jesus, my only Hope, grant me Thy grace,
Teach me in joy and pain Thy hand to trace;
Keep Thou my heart in peace, bid ev'ry murmur cease,
Come and my faith increase, Savior, in Thee.

-FANNY CROSBY

HOPE IN PRAYER

The LORD came and stood and called as at other times, "Samuel! Samuel!" And Samuel said, "Speak, for Your servant is listening."

1 SAMUEL 3:10 NASB

When we wait upon God in prayer, we demonstrate hope in His grace and goodness to answer and bless us. The Israelites used to have to hear God's words from a prophet. But after Christ's death and resurrection, and with the Holy Spirit in our lives, we can approach God in prayer directly. Thomas á Kempis prays, along with Samuel, to hear from God personally.

The children of Israel once said to Moses, "Speak to us yourself and we will listen; but let not God speak to us, or we will die" (Exodus 20:19 NASB). I won't pray this way, LORD. Rather with Samuel the prophet, I ask humbly and earnestly, "Speak, LORD, for Your servant is listening."

Don't let Moses or any of the prophets speak to me. I want You to speak to me, God. You inspired and enlightened all the prophets. You alone can instruct me perfectly. And they can do nothing without You.

They can utter fine words, but they cannot give Your Spirit. They do indeed speak beautifully, but if You remain silent they cannot inflame my heart. They deliver the message; You give understanding. They place before us mysteries, but You unlock their meaning. They proclaim commandments; You help us to keep them. They point out the way; You give strength for the journey. They work only outwardly; You instruct and enlighten our hearts. They water the seed, but You make it grow. They cry out words, and You give understanding to the hearer.

Let not Moses speak to me, therefore, but You, the LORD my God, everlasting truth. Speak in case I die and remain barren when I am merely given outward advice and am not lit from within. I don't want to be judged because I have heard the word, and not kept it; known it, but not loved it; and believed it, but not obeyed it.

Speak, therefore, LORD, for Your servant listens. "You have the words of eternal life" (John 6:68 NKJV). Speak to me for the comfort of my soul. Revise my life for Your praise, Your glory, and Your everlasting honor. Amen.

-THOMAS Á KEMPIS

> *Speak, O blessèd Master,*
> *In this quiet hour,*
> *Let me see Thy face, LORD,*
> *Feel Thy touch of power.*

-EMILY MAY GRIMES

TRUST AND OBEY

Trust in the LORD, and do good; dwell in the land,
and feed on His faithfulness.

PSALM 37:3 NKJV

Just as Meister Eckhart says, "Do exactly what you would do if you felt most secure," we should also follow God without fear of the outcome, and then we will be secure. The security comes at the beginning and end of each decision. When we act as if we were secure, then we do the right thing, and then we will feel secure because we obeyed. The more we step out in trust, the more our trust in God will grow.

When we obey God and take a step of faith, He will never let us down. God will always look out for us and keep His promises. Thomas á Kempis encourages obedience and faithful action in spite of doubting or fear of difficult consequences.

If you continue faithful and diligent in doing, God will undoubtedly be faithful and generous in rewarding. Continue to have reasonable hope of gaining salvation, but do not act as though you were certain of it for fear that you will grow apathetic and proud.

One day when a certain man who wavered often and anxiously between hope and fear was struck with sadness, he knelt in humble prayer before the altar of a church. While meditating on these things, he said, "Oh, if I only knew whether I should make it to the end!"

Instantly he heard God's answer within his heart, "If you knew this, what would you do? Do now what you would do then, and you will be quite secure." Immediately consoled and comforted, he resigned himself to following God's will; and his anxious uncertainty ceased. His curiosity no longer sought to know what the future held for him, and he tried instead to find the perfect, the acceptable will of God in the beginning and end of each good deed.

Dread of difficulty keeps many from eagerly improving their lives. Certainly those who try bravely to overcome the most difficult and unpleasant obstacles far outdo others in the pursuit of virtue. A person makes the most progress and deserves the most grace precisely in those matters where they gain the greatest victories over self. True, each one has their own difficulties to meet and conquer, but a person who is diligently and enthusiastically seeking virtue will make greater progress even though they have more passion to subdue than one who is more naturally even-tempered but less concerned about virtue.

-THOMAS Á KEMPIS

If we will seek God with all our heart, soul, and strength, it doesn't matter how weak and tempted to sin we are. God used Jacob, the trickster, because Jacob sought Him and wouldn't let go until God blessed him. God uses those who seek His heart, not those who are perfect and don't think they need Him. May God place a desire in our hearts that won't be filled by anything but Him.

> *Put thou thy trust in God,*
> *In duty's path go on;*
> *Walk in His strength with faith and hope,*
> *So shall thy work be done.*

-PAUL GERHARDT

A STEADY HOPE

The one who doubts is like the surf of the sea, driven and tossed by the wind. For that man ought not to expect that he will receive anything from the LORD.

Every Christian has doubts at one time or another. Having doubts isn't a sin, just as having temptations isn't a sin. Jesus had both temptations and doubts. However, we cannot give in to our doubts. If we let doubts take over our thoughts and our actions, then we're immobilized. Hannah Whitall Smith explains that God can't work in us or through us until we give our doubts to Him.

The whole root and cause then of our wavering Christian experience is not, as we may have thought, our sins, but is simply and only our doubts. Doubts create an impassable gulf between our souls and the LORD, just as inevitably as they do between us and our earthly friends; and no amount of fervor or earnestness can bridge this gulf in one case any more than in the other.

This is not because God is angry, and vents His displeasure in this way on the person who doubts, but it is because of that inherent nature of things that makes it impossible for doubt and confidence to exist together, whether in earthly relations or heavenly.

The Israelites could not enter in the Promised Land because

of their unbelief. (See Numbers 14:22-23; Hebrews 3:18.) It was not that God would not allow them to enter in as a punishment for their unbelief, but they simply could not. It was an impossibility. Faith is the only door into the kingdom of Heaven, and there is no other.

To effectively walk in faith we must lay our doubts, just as we lay our other sins, upon God's altar, and make a total surrender of them. We must give up all freedom to doubt, and must consecrate our power of believing to Him, and must trust Him to keep us trusting. We must make our faith in His Word as inevitable and necessary a thing as is our obedience to His will. We must be as loyal to our heavenly Friend as we are to our earthly friends, and must refuse to recognize the possibility of such thing as any questioning or doubting of His love or His faithfulness.

-HANNAH WHITALL SMITH

In doubt and temptation I rest, LORD, in Thee;
My hand is in Thy hand, Thou carest for me;
My soul with Thy counsel through life Thou wilt guide,
And afterward make me in glory abide.

-AUTHOR UNKNOWN

THE GIFT OF GOD'S SON

Jesus said, . . . "This is how much God loved the world: He gave his Son,
his one and only Son. And this is why: so that no one need be destroyed;
by believing in him, anyone can have a whole and lasting life."

JOHN 3:10,16 MSG

Sometimes Christians tend to focus on Christ's sacrifice on
the cross and forget about the other gifts and blessings God gave
us through His Son. Just as God didn't just create people and
leave them to fend for themselves, Christ didn't just die on the
cross, consider us forgiven, and leave. Andrew Murray thanks
God for the gift of His Son, who not only saved us, but also lives
in us, guides us, and transforms us.

God gave Christ, in His birth as a human, in order to be forever one with us. He gave Him, in His death on the cross as a
guarantee, in order to take our sin upon Himself. He gave Him
on the throne of heaven, in order to arrange for our welfare, as our
Representative and Intercessor over all the powers of heaven.
And, He gave Him in the outpouring of the Spirit, in order to
dwell in us, to be entirely and altogether our own. (See Romans
8:32,34; 1 John 4:9-10.)

Yes; this is the love of God, that He gave His Son to us, for
us, in us. He gave nothing less than His Son Himself. This is the
love of God; not that He gives us something, but that He gives us
someone—a living person—not one or another blessing, but

Him in whom is all life and blessing—Jesus Himself. Not simply forgiveness, or revival, or sanctification, or glory does He give us; but Jesus, His own Son.

The LORD Jesus is the beloved, the equal, the best friend, the eternal blessing of the Father. And it is the will of the Father that we should have Jesus as ours, even as God has Him. (See John 17:23,25.) For this purpose He gave Him to us. The whole of salvation consists in this: to have, to possess, and to enjoy Jesus. God has given His Son, given Him completely to become ours.

What have we, then, to do? To take Him, to receive and to use for ourselves the gift of God, to enjoy Jesus as our own. This is eternal life for "He who has the Son has life" (1 John 5:12 NKJV).

-ANDREW MURRAY

The greatest gift of God is the relationship we have with Him through His Son, Jesus. Jesus is the answer to all our problems. When we're frustrated and scared, all we need to do is turn to Him. Our lives will be transformed with a foundational joy that flows from His presence and His love.

My counsel for you is simple and straightforward: Just go ahead with what you've been given. You received Christ Jesus, the Master; now live him.

COLOSSIANS 2:6 MSG

GOD IS LOVE

God is love. This is how God showed his love among us:
He sent his one and only Son into the world that we might live through
him. This is love: not that we loved God, but that he loved us and sent
his Son as an atoning sacrifice for our sins.

1 JOHN 4:8-10 NIV

R. A. Torrey tells how with just three words, "God is love," a
lost man can find Christ.

"God is love" (1 John 4:8 NIV). That sums up the whole contents of the Bible. The Bible is simply God's love story, the story
of the love of a holy God to a sinful world. That is the most
amazing thing in the Bible. People tell us the Bible is full of things
that are impossible to believe. I know of nothing else so impossible to believe as that a holy God should love a sinful world, and
should love such individuals as you and me, as the Bible says He
does. But impossible as it is to believe, it is true. There is mighty
power in that one short sentence, power to break the hardest
heart, power to reach individual men and women who are sunk
down in sin, and to lift them up until they are fit for a place
beside the LORD Jesus Christ upon the Throne.

One stormy night, before the time of the church meeting, the
door stood ajar. A man partly intoxicated saw it open, and
thought he might go in and get warm. He did not know what
sort of a place it was, but when he pushed the door open he saw
the text blazing out, "God is love."

He pulled the door closed, and walked away muttering to himself, "God is not love. If God is love, He would love me. God does not love a wretch like me." But it kept on burning down into his soul, "God is love! God is love! God is love!"

After a while he went back and took a seat in a corner. When the pastor, Dwight L. Moody, walked down after the meeting, he found the man weeping like a child.

"What is the trouble?" he asked. "What was it in the sermon that touched you?"

"I didn't hear a word of your sermon."

"Well, what is the trouble?"

"That text up there."

Mr. Moody sat down and from his Bible showed him the way of life, and he was saved.

-R. A. TORREY

If you get overwhelmed with guilt, and doubts of God's mercy take over, repeat to yourself the assurance, "God is love!"

> Let every soul from sin awake,
> Let every heart sweet music make,
> And sing with us for Jesus' sake:
> God is love!

-EDMUND S. LORENZ

TRUE CHRISTIANITY

Have you lost your senses?
After starting your Christian lives in the Spirit,
why are you now trying to become perfect by your own human effort?

GALATIANS 3:3 NLT

In the sixteenth century, Teresa of Avila (1515-1582) said, "From silly devotions and from sour-faced saints, good LORD, deliver us." This prayer applies today more than ever.

There are many Christians who aren't living as if they are free in Christ. Instead, they're still slaves, bound by either sin or the law. It is obvious to unbelievers that they lead strict and unhappy lives or that they are living a lie, worshiping God on Sundays but during the week doing whatever they want.

Many nonbelievers use the hypocrisy and unhappiness of modern Christians, who follow empty rituals but don't lead changed lives, to excuse their own rebellion of God. But to base our denial of Christ on the actions of other people is just an excuse. People have always been sinning and turning away from a forgiving and loving God. It's like someone saying they don't want to be a politician because most politicians are corrupt. If everyone thought like that, there would be no improvement in government at all, and we would all suffer.

We need to judge God as himself and not use the mistakes of His servants as our guide. God has always been true. He keeps reaching out to us as we keep turning away. He forgives over and over and returns our curses with blessings. He is the good

Shepherd who will search for the lost sheep and scattered sheep. He will bandage and heal the hurt and lead us from the darkness into the good land. (See Ezekiel 34.)

Deciding not to follow God leads to more personal consequences than just deciding not to be a politician. Those who don't follow God are slaves to sin whether they know it or not. They miss out on the true freedom that comes from God. And ultimately, they miss out on an eternity spent with God in paradise.

François Fenelon says that it is our job, then, to seek God's grace and go where it leads, rather than to get bogged down in the practices of religion.

We should not think lightly, therefore, of the grace of God, as shown in that inferior form of religion that stops short of the more glorious and perfected form of pure love. We are to follow God's grace, and not to go before it. To the higher state of pure love we are to advance step by step; watching carefully God's inward and outward providence; and receiving increased grace by improving the grace we have, till the dawning light becomes the perfect day.

-FRANÇOIS FENELON

True Christianity is a relationship between people and the God who made them. It is made possible by the grace of God, the sacrifice of Jesus, and the power of the Holy Spirit. It all flows from God. The more you seek Him, the more you will desire to change, and the more you will be changed.

HUMBLE TO RECEIVE GRACE

[Jesus] told his next story, . . . "The Pharisee posed and prayed like this:
'Oh, God, I thank you that I am not like other people—robbers, crooks,
adulterers, or, heaven forbid, like this tax man.' Meanwhile the tax man,
slumped in the shadows, his face in his hands, not daring to look up,
said, 'God, give mercy. Forgive me, a sinner.'" Jesus commented,
"This tax man, not the other, went home made right with God.
If you walk around with your nose in the air, you're going to
end up flat on your face, but if you're content to be simply yourself,
you will become more than yourself."

LUKE 18:9,11,13-14 MSG

Sometimes praying is easy. We desire to spend time with
God, and we immediately sense His love and spend hours with
Him delighting in His presence. But other times prayer is difficult. We sit down to approach God and soon become distracted
and feel like God isn't there and isn't listening. It is in these times
that we realize that our confidence needs to be in God's grace
toward us, not in our ability to pray or to reach Him. Thomas á
Kempis warns us against trusting and depending on our feelings
in prayer. When praying is easy, it isn't necessarily because of us,
and when it is hard, it isn't necessarily because of us. We should-
n't congratulate or berate ourselves on our feelings in prayer. We
could be confident and "spiritual" like the proud Pharisee, and still
not reach God. Just because we don't feel God there, blessing us,
doesn't mean that He isn't.

It is better and safer for you to hide the grace of devotion, not to be excited by it, not to speak or think much of it. Instead you can humble yourself and fear in case you are unworthy of it. Do not cling too closely to this strong feeling, for it may quickly be changed to the opposite.

When you are living in grace, think how miserable and needy you are without it. Your progress in spiritual life does not consist in having the grace of comfort, but in enduring its withdrawal with humility, resignation, and patience, so that you neither become listless in prayer nor neglect your other duties in the least; but on the contrary do what you can do as well as you know how, and do not neglect yourself completely because of your dryness or anxiety of mind.

-THOMAS Á KEMPIS

If our confidence is in us, then we will fail. Our desires for God and our enjoyment of prayer will always go up and down. It is only when our confidence is in God that we can keep going in prayer without the help of our encouraging feelings. Our faith and trust is in a God who will reward us with His grace when we seek Him, whether we feel "spiritual" or not.

Let us then approach the throne of grace with confidence, so that we may receive mercy and find grace to help us in our time of need.

HEBREWS 4:16 NIV

REJOICING IN THE HOPE OF GOD'S WORD

[The LORD said,] "Behold, I am with you and will keep you wherever you go, . . . for I will not leave you until I have done what I have promised you."

GENESIS 28:15 NASB

Christian hope is more than a feeling, desire, or belief. It is more than the cheerful optimism that keeps us going. Christian hope is a firm and active trust that is based on the promises of God. We live in hope when we expect God to be loving and amazing and to do what He says He will. In his hymn "Arise My Soul," Charles Wesley invites us to "rejoice in hope" by resting on the promises of God's Holy Word.

The Word of God is sure,
And never can remove;
We shall in heart be pure
And perfected in love.

Then let us gladly bring
Our sacrifice of praise;
Let us give thanks and sing
And glory in His grace.
Rejoice in hope, rejoice with me;

Rejoice in hope, rejoice with me.
We shall from all our sins be free.

-CHARLES WESLEY

We shall be like Christ. When we live in heaven, we will shed our sinful desires along with our earthly bodies. We will rest in Christ completely. We will be full of true joy and display God's glory and love. Rejoice in hope!

HOPE IN
GOD'S TIMING

The LORD longs to be gracious to you, and therefore He waits on
high to have compassion on you. For the LORD is a God of justice;
How blessed are all those who long for Him.

ISAIAH 30:18 NASB

How frustrating it is to wait. It is one thing to wait in a slow
line, but it is quite another thing to wait for a new job. Or what
about those who have to wait for an organ transplant? It is not
just patience they need, but hope. Andrew Murray says that God
always has a reason for waiting to act to answer our prayers. He
cares for us and is never too late.

You ask, "How is it, if God waits to be gracious, that even
after I come and wait upon Him, He does not give the help I
seek, but waits on longer and longer?" Part of the reason for the
wait is that God is a wise farmer, who "waits for the precious pro-
duce of the soil, being patient about it" (James 5:7 NASB). He cannot gather the fruit until it is ripe. He knows when we are spiritually ready to receive the blessing for our profit and His glory.

Waiting in the sunshine of His love is what will ripen the
soul for His blessing. Waiting under the cloud of trial, which ends
in showers of blessing, is just as important. Be assured that if God

waits longer than you could wish, it is only to make the blessing twice as valuable. God waited four thousand years, until the right time, before He sent His Son.

Our times are in His hands. He will avenge His chosen ones quickly. He will make haste to help us, and won't delay one hour too long.

-ANDREW MURRAY

THE GRACE TO PRAY

Men and women don't live by bread only;
we live by every word that comes from GOD's mouth.

DEUTERONOMY 8:3 MSG

Just as physical food gives us energy to work physically, God's Word gives us the spiritual food to work spiritually. If we want to start a difficult or long physical task, we prepare by eating a healthy, filling meal. It is the same when we face a spiritual task. We need to first eat the bread of God. Preacher and orphanage founder George Müller explains how the power, ability, or grace to pray comes from God, specifically from the careful reading of His Word.

Now what is the food for the soul? Not prayer, but the Word of God. We don't simply read the Word of God, so that it only passes through our minds like water through a pipe, but we consider what we read, ponder over it, and apply it to our hearts.

When we pray, we speak to God. Now, prayer, in order to be continued for any length of time in other than a formal manner, requires strength or holy desire. Therefore, the time when this exercise of the soul [prayer] can be most effectively performed is after the soul has been nourished by meditation on the Word of God.

In meditation we find our Father speaking to us to encourage us, to comfort us, to instruct us, to humble us, and to reprove us.

We then profitably meditate, with God's blessing, even when we are weak spiritually. Actually, the weaker we are, the more we need meditation for the strengthening of our soul.

-GEORGE MÜLLER

Not only will God's Word give us energy to pray, but it will also teach us how to pray. As we begin to read Scripture and meditate lovingly on God's Word and His amazing character, we will naturally slip into prayer. Every verse and sometimes every word can lead into praise, thanksgiving, confession, and requests for help.

GOD'S GRACE
AND CREATIVITY

Out of the ground the LORD God formed every beast of the field and
every bird of the sky, and brought them to the man to see what he
would call them; and whatever the man called a living creature,
that was its name. The man gave names to all the cattle,
and to the birds of the sky, and to every beast of the field.

GENESIS 2:19-20 NASB

God did not intend for us to be slaves or robots. Instead, from
the very beginning, God created us to be creative like Him. He
made the earth magnificently unique from deserts to rainforests
to snow-capped mountains. And then God had Adam name each
and every one of the animals and birds. There are over 9,000
species of birds alone. Can you imagine the creativity involved for
God to design each of them, and then for Adam to name them?

God is the source of our creativity. We were made in His
image. He didn't just make us and go on vacation, leaving us on
earth to struggle all on our own. Instead, God delights in inspir-
ing us and giving us dreams. When we plan, we aren't to go off on
our own, thinking we don't need God's help or inspiration,
because then we will miss out on great adventures and blessings.
And when we think we almost understand everything, He will
wow us again with another angle of His personality through

glimpses of our own soul, other people's actions, and His vibrant creation.

> "If you want to make God laugh,
> tell Him your plans."
>
> -AUTHOR UNKNOWN

If you want to make God smile and help,
ask Him for directions.

CREATIVE HOPE

*I know the thoughts and plans that I have for you, says the LORD,
thoughts and plans for welfare and peace and not for evil, to give you
hope in your final outcome.*

JEREMIAH 29:11 AMP

Madeleine L'Engle writes that "artistic temperament sometimes seems a battleground, a dark angel of destruction and a
bright angel of creativity wrestling." When we sit down to dream,
to write, paint, design, or play, there are two things fighting
against hopeful creativity. The first "dark angel" is our own pride.
We will run ahead, designing ahead of God, and miss out on
wonderful opportunities for Him to show us what we can really
do with Him as our guide.

The second "dark angel" is Satan. He will attempt to convince
us that whatever we are attempting to dream will never come to
completion. Because of his discouragement, we'll start out with
magnificent ideas and images, and end up with practical, boring
skeletons down on paper.

There are two sides to most people. The first is hopeful ideal-
ism that gets excited easily. This side tends to quickly fall in love
with new people, ideas, and plans. It reaches high and often falls
down hard. The second side is hard realism. It fights hard to
squash and thwart the ideas and enthusiasm of the hopeful side.
It says, "You'll only get hurt again. Don't even think about trying
THAT!" And really, it is out for its own good.

But we can't act like emotional toddlers the rest of our lives, grabbing at whatever toy is in front of us. And we also shouldn't be cold, dead people who never attempt anything new and don't even trust to receive the gifts that God has promised. Both of these sides of our personalities are good when they balance each other out. They keep us ready to try some new things but also aware of the consequences.

We don't want to be afraid to jump, because God's plans usually require extreme leaps of trust. We don't want to try every good idea that comes our way, only the ones that God has planned for us.

O God, let us dream big. But let us hold on loosely to our dreams because Your ideas and plans are bigger than we can imagine. We want to be ready and available when You call on us to take the next step. Keep us willing and waiting. Amen.

REPENT AND ACCEPT GOD'S GRACE

The sorrow that is according to the will of God produces
a repentance without regret, leading to salvation,
but the sorrow of the world produces death.

2 CORINTHIANS 7:10 NASB

Repentance in the Bible is not just a feeling. It is an action. Remorse is a feeling. If we repent, we turn away from sin. Christ came to call sinners to repentance. (See Luke 5:32.) Remorse often leads to repentance, but isn't necessary. Charles Spurgeon explains that our guilt for not "feeling repentant" is false, and we can focus on the love of Christ instead of feeling guilty for not feeling guilty.

Remember that the person who truly repents is never satisfied with their own repentance. We can no more repent perfectly than we can live perfectly. However pure our tears, there will always be some dirt in them: There will be something to be repented of even in our best repentance.

But listen! To repent is to change your mind about sin, and Christ, and all the great things of God. There is sorrow implied in this; but the main point is the turning of the heart from sin to Christ. If there is this turning, then you have the essence of true repentance, even though you have no hint of alarm or despair in your mind.

-CHARLES SPURGEON

Instead of being caught in a cycle of blame and guilt, we can stop and turn to God and accept His love and power to break the power of habitual sin in our life.

> *I've wandered far away from God,*
> *Now I'm coming home;*
> *The paths of sin too long I've trod,*
> *LORD, I'm coming home.*

-WILLIAM J. KIRKPATRICK

THE GROWTH
OF GRACE

*Because your faith is greatly enlarged, and the love of each one
of you toward one another grows ever greater; therefore, we ourselves
speak proudly of you among the churches of God for your perseverance
and faith in the midst of all your persecutions and
afflictions which you endure.*

2 THESSALONIANS 1:3-4 NASB

Mark Twain once said, "It ain't the parts of the Bible that I
can't understand that bother me, it is the parts that I do understand." We can take that to mean that there are plenty of clear and
understandable parts of the Bible that will bother us and require
our changed behavior and obedience. George Müller warns us to
keep ourselves close to God without doing things we know are
wrong. He explains that the way to grow faith and to experience a
life of God's blessings is to keep our account with God clean. We
will short-circuit the many blessings that come from a life of faith
if we are full of guilt. And then we will miss the opportunity for
His help.

It is of the utmost importance that we seek to maintain an
honest heart and a good conscience. Therefore we shouldn't
knowingly and habitually indulge in those things that are contrary
to the mind of God. This is particularly important with reference
to our growth in faith.

How can I possibly continue to act with faith in God, in any situation, if I am habitually grieving Him? How can I seek to detract from the glory and honor of Him of whom I say I trust, upon whom I say I depend? All my confidence in God, all my leaning upon Him in the hour of trial, will be gone if I have a guilty conscience, and do not seek to put it away, but still continue to do things which are contrary to the mind of God.

And if, in any particular situation, I cannot trust in God because of my guilty conscience, then my faith is weakened by my distrust. With every fresh trial, faith either increases by trusting God, and therefore getting help, or it decreases by not trusting Him. Then there is less and less power to look simply and directly to Him, and our habit of self-dependence is born or encouraged. One or the other of these will always be the case in each trial of faith.

Either we trust in God, and in that case we neither trust in ourselves, nor in others, nor in circumstances, nor in anything else; or we do trust in one or more of these, and in that case do not trust in God.

-GEORGE MÜLLER

Because of our pride, it's always hard to give up a bad habit, turn from sin, or even turn from something that's distracting us from God. But when we refuse to obey, we effectively bar God from blessing with His grace and leading us into a deeper relationship with Him.

Let us turn from everything that hinders the abundant grace of God from filling our lives with His many blessings.

WAIT, HOPE, AND EXPECT

I wait for the LORD, I expectantly wait, and in His word do I hope.

PSALM 130:5 AMP

The Spanish verb *esperar* has three meanings: to wait, to hope, and to expect. So when you "esperar" on God, it can imply all three meanings at once. Waiting is an action, and hoping and expecting are attitudes. George Müller, who was famous for his faith in God's provision, writes that the only way to have God strengthen your faith is to hope and expect and, therefore, wait for His perfect solution.

To let God strengthen our faith, we need to let God work for us. When the hour of the test comes, we shouldn't figure out a solution of our own. When God gives faith, it is for the purpose of being tested and increased.

However weak our faith may be, God will try it. The test only has this restriction; God leads us on and tests our faith gently, gradually, and patiently. At first, our faith will be tested very little in comparison with what it may be later. For God never lays more upon us than He gives us strength to bear.

Now, when the testing of faith comes, we are naturally inclined to distrust God, and to trust rather in ourselves, our friends, or our circumstances. We would rather figure out a solution of our own, than to simply look to God and wait for His help.

But if we do not patiently wait for God's help, if we work a solution of our own, then at the next testing of our faith it will be the same again. We will be disposed to deliver ourselves. Then, with every fresh occasion of testing, our faith will decrease.

On the contrary, if we were to stand still in order to see the salvation of God, we would see His hand stretched out on our behalf. When we trusted in Him alone, our faith would be increased. And with every fresh case where the hand of God is stretched out on our behalf in the testing of our faith, our faith would be increased more.

For the believer to have their faith strengthened, they must, especially, give time to God, who tests their faith in order to prove to His child, in the end, how willing He is to help and deliver them, the moment it is good for them.

-GEORGE MÜLLER

GOD'S GRACE
REVEALS OUR SIN

*I know that nothing good dwells within me. . . . O unhappy and pitiable
and wretched man that I am! Who will release and deliver me from [the
shackles of] this body of death? O thank God! [He will!] through Jesus
Christ (the Anointed one) our LORD!*

ROMANS 7:18, 24-25 AMP

John Bunyan explains how there are two steps of God revealing our unworthiness to us. The first is when we find out what
miserable sinners we are without Christ and decide to turn to
Him for our salvation. But the second is when we find out that
we aren't good saints without Christ either. We need God, not
only to keep us from sinning, but also to make us able to act in
love and shine with His glory.

God will mercifully follow a sinner, and show them the short-
ness of their actions, the emptiness of their duties, and the
uncleanness of their righteousness. God intends and arranges salvation of their soul; for they shall by gospel light be wearied out
of everything. They shall be made to see the vanity of everything,
and that only the personal righteousness of Jesus Christ is
ordained by God to save the sinner from the due reward of their
sins.

But watch the sinner now, who at the sight and sense of their own nothingness falls into a kind of despair; for although they believe in salvation—through the deception of their own good opinion of themself—they still don't have a good opinion of the grace of God in the righteousness of Christ. Then they conclude that if salvation is alone from the grace of God through the righteousness of Christ, and all of people's actions are utterly rejected as to the justification of their person with God, then they are cast away.

Now, the reason of this sinking of heart is the sight that God has given them—a sight of the uncleanness of their best performance. The former sight of their immoralities did somewhat distress them, and make them commit to their own good deeds to ease their conscience. Therefore this was their prop, their foundation. But now God has taken this from under them, and now they fall. Therefore their best also abandons them, and flies away like the morning dew.

-JOHN BUNYAN

O God, we are nothing without You. Give us the courage and faith to give up trying to be good on our own. We want to be dead to sin and alive to Christ. Let us each day live more and more in You. Amen.

Hope in God's Guidance

[Jesus] was withdrawn from them about a stone's throw, and He knelt down and prayed, saying, "Father, if it is Your will, take this cup away from Me; nevertheless not My will, but Yours, be done."

Luke 22:41-42 NKJV

The life of Christ was unique. He didn't decide to be crucified based on His desire or opinion—for clearly He didn't want to die a painful death. He didn't use critical thinking or the wise advice of His friends to make His decision to go to the cross without a fight—for logically Christ could have fought off the soldiers with the help of Peter and the disciples. Or He could have at least argued back at His trial. Christ never had problems winning debates with the Pharisees before. His close friend betrayed Him, there was a conspiracy to kill Him, and the witnesses at His trial were false. Logically, Christ should have fought back somehow.

Christ also didn't decide to go to the cross based on tradition, because traditionally God fought on the side of His righteous followers. God's prophets were used to the odds not being in their favor. For example, Elijah's standoff to show Israel that they should follow the LORD instead of Baal was just him and God against 450 pagan priests. (See 1 Kings 18.)

But Christ decided to go to the cross by waiting, listening, and submitting His will to the Father. And His listening obedience blessed all the peoples of the earth with the opportunity to conquer sin and follow God. Friends, logic, and tradition did not point to the cross. They also were unable and blind to the hope of the resurrection.

Jesus listened to the Father's promise that He would die, face the burden of mankind's sins, and then rise again with the power and ability to live in people and change their hearts one-on-one.

Just as Christ submitted His will to God's will, so we should also turn to God for guidance. He will bless us with the hope of His amazing plans and the grace of His presence.

TO BE ONE WITH GOD

Jesus spoke these things;. . . "The glory which You have given Me
I have given to them, that they may be one, just as We are one;
I in them and You in Me, that they may be perfected in unity,
so that the world may know that You sent Me, and loved them,
even as You have loved Me."

JOHN 17:1,22-23 NASB

God's grace means that not only can we have a relationship with Him, but that we can be one with Him as Jesus and He are one. As we submit our will to God's amazing and perfect will, we will know His love. The writer of the *Theologia Germanica* writes that we cannot have God's will by our own striving or works, but it is a gift from God.

In what does our union with God consist? It means that we should be purely, simply, and completely at one with the one eternal Will of God, or altogether without our own will, so that our created will should flow out into the eternal Will and be swallowed up and lost in it, so that God's eternal Will alone should make the decision about what we should do or not do.

Religious exercises cannot do this, nor words, nor works, nor any person or work done by a person. We must therefore give up and renounce all things, suffering them to be what they are, and enter into union with God. Yet the outward things must continue. Sleeping and waking, walking and standing still, speaking and being silent, must go on as long as we live.

But when this union truly comes to pass and is established, the inner person from now on stands still in this union. As for the outer person, God allows them to be moved here and there, from this to that, among things which are necessary and right. So the outer person says sincerely, "I have no wish to be or not to be, to live or die, to know or be ignorant, to do or leave undone. I am ready for all that is to be or ought to be, and obedient to whatever I have to do or suffer." Thus the outer person has no purpose except to do their part to further the eternal Will.

As for the inner person, it is truly perceived that they shall stand still, though the outer person needs to be moved. And if the inner person has any explanation of the actions of the outer person, they say only that such things that are decided by the eternal Will must be and ought to be. It is like this when God Himself dwells in a person; as we plainly see in the case of Christ.

Moreover, where there is this union, which is the outflow of the Divine light and dwells in its beams, there is no spiritual pride nor boldness of spirit, but unbounded humility and a lowly broken heart; there is also an honest and blameless walk, justice, peace, contentment, and every virtue. Where these are missing, there is no true union. For even as nothing can bring about or further this union, so nothing can spoil or hinder it, except the person themself with their self-will.

-THEOLOGIA GERMANICA

God, I submit my will to Yours. With each step I take in obedience to You, my faith and trust in You will grow stronger. I want to be one with You and spend time fully in Your presence. Amen.

"Whoever possesses God in their being, has Him in a divine manner, and He shines out to them in all things; for them all things taste of God and in all things it is God's image that they see."

-MEISTER ECKHART

JESUS TRANSCENDS
THE LAW

What the Law could not do, weak as it was through the flesh, God did:
sending His own Son in the likeness of sinful flesh and as an offering
for sin, He condemned sin in the flesh, so that the requirement of the
Law might be fulfilled in us, who do not walk according to the flesh
but according to the Spirit.

ROMANS 8:3-4 NASB

Our salvation is more than a To Do list that we try to check off to please God. The evangelist and Salvation Army cofounder, Catherine Booth, passionately explains how knowing what is right and trying to do good cannot save us; only Christ can save us.

Where does the Law fail us? It does all this for me: It brings me right up opening my eyes, creating an intense desire after holiness and the effort behind it, and then it just fails me. Where? At the essential point. It cannot give me power. That is where the Law fails. It cannot give me power to fulfill itself.

Oh! But there is a Gospel these days, a Law—Gospel. A great deal of the Gospel these days never gets any further than the Law, and some people tell me that it is never intended to do so. Then I ask, "How then does Christ Jesus help me? How am I better for such a Gospel, if my Gospel cannot deliver me from the power of sin? If through the Gospel I cannot get deliverance from this "I-would-if-I-could religion," this "Oh-wretched-man-that-I-am religion," how am I benefited by it? (See Romans 7:24.)

How does your Gospel do more for me than the Law? The Law convinced me of sin, and set me desiring and longing after righteousness; but where is the superiority of Jesus Christ, if He cannot lead me further than that? And I say, "Very well; your faith is vain, and Christ died in vain, and you are yet in your sins, if that is all it can do." If that is all Jesus Christ can do, His coming is vain, and I am yet in my sins, and am doomed to hug this dead corpse to the last, and go down to hell; for death will never do for me what the blood and sacrifice of Jesus Christ cannot do for me. If Christ cannot supersede the Law, then I am lost, and lost for ever.

Oh! but the real Gospel does. The Gospel that represents Jesus Christ, not as a system of truth to be received, into the mind, as I should receive a system of philosophy, or astronomy, but it represents Him as a real, living, mighty Savior, able to save me now.

-CATHERINE BOOTH

The gospel of Christ transcends the gospel of law. A relationship with Christ, our Savior, is the only thing that can purify us and set us free from our lives of sin and emptiness. The way to Christ's freedom is saying, "I am a sinner; and I cannot be pure no matter how hard I try. I need You, Christ, to save me and give me

Your Spirit to empower, purify, and guide me. I give up. Take over. I give my life to You now."

It is only this relationship with Christ, who was sinless and yet died for us, that can save us from the judgment of the law. Praise God for His mercy and loving kindness that never fails, but always forgives and brings us freedom!

A New Identity

Behold what manner of love the Father has bestowed on us,
that we should be called children of God!

1 John 3:1-2 NKJV

R. A. Torrey's sermon on identity mentions that one of the greatest graces that God has given to us is the new identity as His very own children.

Oh, that wondrous gift that God bestowed upon you and me, that men and women like us should be called children of God! Oh, what love!

Suppose on his coronation day King Edward, after all the ceremonies were over, had taken his carriage of state, and had ridden down to the East End of London, and had seen some ragged, wretched, profane boy, utterly uneducated and morally corrupt. Suppose his great heart of love had gone out to that boy, and, stepping up to that poor wanderer, he had said, "I love you. I am going to take you in my carriage to the palace. I am going to dress you fit to be a king's son, and you shall be known as the son of King Edward the Seventh." Would it not have been wonderful?

But it would not have been so wonderful as that the infinitely holy God should have looked down upon you and me in our filthiness and rags and depravity, and that He should have so loved us that He should have called us to be the children of God.

-R. A. Torrey

Remind yourself as you go through your day that you are a child of God. Think about what that means in your present circumstances.

> Blessèd are the sons of God,
> They are bought with Christ's own blood;
> They are ransomed from the grave,
> Life eternal they shall have;
> With them numbered may we be,
> Here and in eternity.

-JOSEPH HUMPHREYS

OUR HOPE
IS IN GOD

Thus says God the LORD, Who created the heavens and
stretched them out, Who spread out the earth and its offspring,
Who gives breath to the people on it and spirit to those who walk in it,
"I am the LORD, I have called You in righteousness,
I will also hold You by the hand and watch over You."

ISAIAH 42:5-6 NASB

God is so amazing. He is large enough to create the universe, and complex and creative enough to design all the different creatures in it. How do we have a relationship with a God who is so large we can't fully comprehend Him? Andrew Murray encourages us to meditate and quietly remember who God is before we pray.

Before you pray, bow quietly before God. Remember and realize who He is, how near He is, and how certainly He can and will help. Just be still before Him, and allow His Holy Spirit to waken and stir in your soul the childlike disposition of absolute dependence and confident expectation.

Wait upon God as a living Being, as the living God, who notices you. He is just longing to fill you with His salvation.

Wait on God until you know you have met Him. Prayer will then become so different.

-ANDREW MURRAY

Even though God is beyond our comprehension, we are not beyond His. He created us, notices us, and loves us. We can be filled with a joyous hope because when we seek Him, we will find Him.

THE ABUSE OF GRACE

What do we do? Keep on sinning so God can keep on forgiving? I should hope not! If we've left the country where sin is sovereign, how can we still live in our old house there? Or didn't you realize we packed up and left there for good?

ROMANS 6:1-2 MSG

There are those who think that forgiveness leads to loose morals and behavior without the fear of punishment. But in fact, forgiveness leads to the opposite, a changed heart and loving behavior.

The character Jean Valjean in Victor Hugo's famous novel *Les Misérables* is one example of the positive results of God's grace. When a pastor forgives him for stealing the silver and gives him the candlesticks too, Valjean changes from a vengeful criminal to an honest and compassionate man who takes care of widows and orphans. (See James 1:27.) God's grace flowing through the pastor changes Valjean.

John Bunyan agrees that the results of grace are always good. God's grace changes and encourages us to overflow with His love to our neighbors and friends.

A self-righteous person, a person of the law, considers grace and mercy their greatest enemy. Never did one fall into harm by the enjoyment and fullness of the grace of God. There is no fear of excess or overindulging here. Grace makes no one proud, no one wanton, no one haughty, no one careless or negligent as to their duty to either God or people.

No, grace keeps people low in their own eyes, humble, self-denying, penitent, watchful, pleasant in good things, charitable: and makes one kindly affectionate to other Christians, pitiful and courteous to all.

-JOHN BUNYAN

When we become aware of the transforming love and acceptance that flows from God, we will fall on our faces with repentance and a desire to seek God further and to help others like God has helped us.

From the fullness of his grace we have all received
one blessing after another.

JOHN 1:16 NIV

POWER OVER SIN IS YOURS!

*[Jesus said], "All authority has been given to Me in heaven
and on earth."*

MATTHEW 28:18 NKJV

The great R. A. Torrey tells this story:

A man came to me one day and began to tell me his life-story.

He said, "Away over in Scotland, when I was but seven years
of age, I started to read the Bible, and I got as far as
Deuteronomy. Reading there I found that if a man kept the whole
law for a hundred years, and then broke the law at any point, he
was under a curse. Is that right?"

I said, "Well, that is about the substance of it."

He continued, "Then I got to the New Testament, and I read
John 3:16: 'God so loved the world that He gave His only begotten Son, that whoever believes in Him should not perish but have
everlasting life' (NKJV). Then I saw that the LORD Jesus had borne
all my sin, and my burden went away. Was I converted?"

I replied, "That sounds like a true conversion."

Then he said, "I am now working down in the stockyards. You
know the stockyards are a very hard neighborhood. I have got
into drinking. I try to break away, but I cannot. Is there any way
to get victory over sin?"

I said, "You only believed half of the Gospel, that Christ died
for our sins according to the Scriptures, and was buried. Will you

now believe the other half of the Gospel? Will you believe that He rose again?"

And he said, "I believe everything that is in the Bible."

"Do you believe what Jesus Christ says in Matthew 28:18, 'All authority has been given to Me in heaven and on earth?'"

"Yes."

"Then He has the authority to set you free from the power of sin. Will you put your trust in Him right now, to do it?"

"I will."

"All right," I said, "let us kneel down." I prayed, and he followed with a prayer something like this, "O God, I believed that Jesus died for my sins on the Cross, and I found peace through believing. Now I believe that Jesus rose again, and that He has all power in Heaven and on earth, and He has got power to set me free today. LORD Jesus, set me free from the power of drink and the power of sin."

In a few weeks I received a letter from that man: "I am so glad I came over to see you. It works!"

Christ has all power in Heaven and on earth, and the devil is no match for Him. The risen Christ has power to snap the chains of alcohol, to snap the chains of drug addiction, to snap the chains of sexual lust, and of every sin; and if you will trust Him to do it for you, He will do it.

-R. A. TORREY (CONDENSED FROM A LARGER PASSAGE)

OUR PART AND GOD'S PART

[Jesus said,] "The Son of Man came to seek and to
save what was lost."

LUKE 19:10 NIV

We have very little to do with the fact that we are Christians.
We accept the forgiveness for our sins and then we accept the
Holy Spirit who gives us the power to obey and keep from sin-
ning again. Sure, obedience, respect, and love are a part of this
acceptance, but it is not the cause of it, only the natural effect of
God's gracious presence. Hannah Whitall Smith emphasizes
God's part in the following story.

A wild young fellow, who was brought to the LORD at a mission meeting, and who became a rejoicing Christian and lived an
exemplary life afterward, was asked by someone what he did to
get converted. "Oh," he said, "I did my part, and the LORD did
His."

"But what was your part," asked the inquirer, "and what was
the LORD's part?"

"My part," was the prompt reply, "was to run away, and the
LORD's part was to run after me until He caught me." A most sig-
nificant answer; but how few can understand it!

God's part is always to run after us. Christ came to seek and
to save that which is lost. "What man among you," He says, "if he
has a hundred sheep and has lost one of them, does not leave the

ninety-nine in the open pasture and go after the one which is lost until he finds it? When he has found it, he lays it on his shoulders, rejoicing" (Luke 15:4-5 NASB).

This is always the divine part; but in our foolishness we do not understand it, but think that the LORD is the one who is lost, and that our part is to seek and find Him. The very expressions we use show this. We urge sinners to "seek the LORD," and we talk about having "found" Him. "Have you found the Savior?" asked a too zealous mission worker of a happy, trusting little girl.

With a look of amazement, she replied in a tone of wonder, "Why, I did not know the Savior was lost!"

-HANNAH WHITALL SMITH

This is true. The Savior is not lost and has never been lost. It is we who have been lost and found. We are the ones who so desperately need a Shepherd.

The Sovereign LORD says: I myself will search for my sheep and look after them. As a shepherd looks after his scattered flock when he is with them, so will I look after my sheep. I will rescue them from all the places where they were. . . . I myself will tend my sheep and have them lie down, declares the Sovereign LORD. I will search for the lost and bring back the strays. I will bind up the injured and strengthen the weak.

EZEKIEL 34:11-12,15-16 NIV

CONFIDENTLY WAITING ON GOD

My soul waits in silence for God only; from Him is my salvation.

PSALM 62:1 NASB

Hope is expecting, desiring, and longing. When we hope for God, our hope is more than a vague desire; it is a firm trusting in His goodness. When we wait in prayer for God we have hope. Waiting displays confidence—confidence that God will come. Andrew Murray implores us to remember that without waiting on God and experiencing His presence daily, we are helpless and hopeless. It is only through prayer that we can experience God's daily saving us and giving us power to do His will.

If salvation truly comes from God and is entirely His work, just as our creation was, then our first and highest duty is to wait on Him and to do that work which pleases Him. Waiting then becomes the only way to the experience of a full salvation—the only way to truly know God as the God of our salvation. All the difficulties which are brought forward, as keeping us back from full salvation, have their cause in this one thing: the lack of knowledge and practice of waiting upon God.

It is then because Christians do not know their relationship to God as absolute poverty and helplessness, that they have no sense of the need of absolute and unceasing dependence, or of the unspeakable blessing of continually waiting on God. But, once we begin to see it and consent to it—that we must, by the Holy

Spirit, each moment receive what God each moment works—waiting on God becomes our brightest hope and joy.

As we begin to understand how God, as God, as infinite Love, delights to impart His own nature to His children as fully as He can—how God is not weary of keeping charge of our life and strength—we wonder why we ever thought that God could not be waited on all day. God unceasingly giving and working and His children unceasingly waiting and receiving; this is the blessed life.

"My soul waits in silence for God only; from Him is my salvation." First, we wait on God for salvation. Then, we learn that salvation is only to bring us to God and teach us to wait on Him. Then, we find what is better still—that waiting on God is itself the highest salvation. It is ascribing to Him the glory of being All; it is experiencing that He is all to us. May God teach us the blessedness of waiting on Him!

-ANDREW MURRAY

AN UNFAILING HOPE

As the deer pants for the water brooks, so pants my soul for You, O God.

PSALM 42:1 NKJV

Our hope of our fulfilled desire is steady and calm. We trust in the Lord, our Rock and our Savior. God does not give us desires and then not fulfill them. And our foundational desire as humans is to be understood, to be loved, and to rest in the amazing presence of our Creator. Frances de Sales refers to this desire as the desire of sovereign good.

This desire [to be always in the presence of God] is just, for who would not desire so desirable a good? But it would be a useless desire, and would be but a continual torment to our heart if we had not assurance that we should at length satisfy it.

The same God which moves in us so passionate a desire, also by a thousand promises made in His Word and His inspirations, gives us assurance, that we may with ease obtain it, provided always that we will to employ the means which He has prepared for us and offers us to this effect.

Now these divine promises and assurances, amazingly, increase the cause of our unrest, by increasing our desire. And yet, while they increase the cause, they undo and destroy the effects. For the assurance which God gives us that paradise is ours, infinitely strengthens the desire we have to enjoy it, and yet weakens, and altogether destroys, the trouble and unrest which this desire brought unto us. Then our hearts by the promises which God has made us, remain quite calmed, and this calm is the root of the most holy virtue which we call hope.

-FRANCES DE SALES

Hope, then, is a desire that is both increased and put at rest by the promises of God. And the more time we spend in God's presence praying, the longer we obey, serve, and depend on Him, the more secure we are in the strength of His promises.

God always provides. He is dependable—our Rock, our firm Foundation, our Shield, our Protector, our Deliverer.

> Lead to the shadow of the Rock of Refuge
> My weary feet;
> Give me the water from the life-stream flowing
> Clear, pure and sweet.
> There from the billows and the tempest hiding,
> Under the shelter of Thy love abiding,
> Safe in the shadow of the "Rock of Ages,"
> Joy shall be mine!

-FANNY CROSBY

In Heavenly Love Abiding

[Jesus said] "Just as the Father has loved Me,
I have also loved you; abide in My love."

JOHN 15:9 NASB

When life gets busy, and we get overwhelmed by the many events that make us feel we are not keeping up, we can pull away for a quiet moment and remember that God loves us. He died for us when we were in rebellion against Him, and even now His love surrounds us in spite of our weakness. Rest in His love today. He is there for you no matter what is going on in your heart or your life.

> *In heavenly love abiding,*
> *No change my heart shall fear;*
> *And safe is such confiding,*
> *For nothing changes here:*
> *The storm may roar without me,*
> *My heart may low be laid;*
> *But God is round about me,*
> *And can I be dismayed?*
>
> *Wherever He may guide me,*
> *No want shall turn me back;*
> *My Shepherd is beside me,*

And nothing can I lack.
His wisdom ever waketh,
His sight is never dim:
He knows the way He taketh,
And I will walk with Him.

Green pastures are before me,
Which yet I have not seen;
Bright skies will soon be o'er me,
Where the dark clouds have been.
My hope I cannot measure:
My path to life is free:
My Savior has my treasure,
And He will walk with me.

-ANNA LAETITIA WARING

THE GRACE OF
GOD'S WORD

*[Jesus said,] "You search the Scriptures because you think
that in them you have eternal life; it is these that testify
[bear witness] about Me; and you are unwilling to come to Me
so that you may have life."*

JOHN 5:39-40 NASB

God's Word is a wonderful grace from Him. In it we can find
truth about Him and begin in some way to understand His heart.
And we must pray for help to understand the Bible. The Word
makes sense to us only as the Holy Spirit opens it up to us; otherwise, it is a closed book whose many passages make no sense.

Although reading your Bible every day will help you to grow
spiritually, don't give in to the temptation to abuse this gift of
God by so focusing on mastering its contents that you forget that
God gave it to you to open your eyes and move your heart to seek
Him.

When you spend time reading the Bible, don't stop there.
Move on to speak to the One who wrote it. Otherwise, your Bible
can become a false idol that causes you to reject the very One who
inspired its writings.

Today as you read your Bible, stop and ask God what He
wants to teach you from the passage before you. Let your time in
the Word be time with Him.

"Christ is the treasure hid in the field of the Scriptures."

-MATTHEW HENRY

THE GIFTS OF THE SPIRIT

There are varieties of gifts, but the same Spirit.

1 CORINTHIANS 12:4 NASB

When the Holy Spirit comes to dwell, each believer can expect to discover new abilities to help the Church and to serve Jesus. These abilities are powered by the Holy Spirit and can only happen with the Spirit's presence.

What are these abilities? For one person it can be the ability to understand God's purposes and His Word and to teach. For another, it can be special knowledge about a person or situation that will enable them to pray with faith for God's will to happen. For some, it may be that they will know what God wants to do and how He wants it done. For another, it may be the ability to build or create beautiful and practical things for the Church. Some may know from someplace deep within where the Holy Spirit dwells just what God wants to say to a person who is struggling. This is not the end of the list of gifts. There are many more listed in 1 Corinthians 12:8-11, Ephesians 4:11, and Romans 12:6-8.

These gifts are not mere natural talents, which any person can have in abundance. The knowledge, understanding, and power that show up when spiritual gifts operate are supernatural in nature. And these special abilities come only to those who belong to God. God even promises that some Christians who lack reputation and status may get greater gifts to create an atmosphere of love and acceptance for them in the Church.

Want to know your spiritual gift? Ask God to show you. Then watch for opportunities to help Christians and to help in church ministry. Be prepared to wait. Some gifts require God to grow the Christian's faith and maturity before the gift will show up. But trust God's promises—it will show up.

THE SOLID ROCK OF HOPE

*[Jesus said]"The rain came down, the streams rose, and the winds blew
and beat against that house; yet it did not fall, because it had
its foundation on the rock."*

MATTHEW 7:25 NIV

Hope based on just anything is worthless. Hope, like faith, is
useless unless it is based on something strong and true. The
Christian preacher Edward Mote set his hope on Christ and only
Christ.

After coming to Christ as a teenager, Mote was a good carpenter and a faithful church member for over thirty years before
his dream of preaching became a reality and he could encourage
others with his sermons and hymns full time. The week after he
wrote the hymn "My Hope is Built," he sang the verses with a
dying woman and her husband during a home prayer time. She
enjoyed the song so much that he left a copy of the song with her,
and then had them printed for others.

The words remind us that when we aren't in control and
things seem to be falling apart, we don't have to worry, because we
base our hope in Christ and His saving actions and loving character.

> *My hope is built on nothing less*
> *Than Jesus' blood and righteousness.*
> *I dare not trust the sweetest frame,*
> *But wholly trust in Jesus' Name.*

When darkness seems to hide His face,
I rest on His unchanging grace.
In every high and stormy gale,
My anchor holds within the veil.

His oath, His covenant, His blood,
Support me in the whelming flood.
When all around my soul gives way,
He then is all my Hope and Stay.

When He shall come with trumpet sound,
Oh, may I then in Him be found.
Dressed in His righteousness alone,
Faultless to stand before the throne.

On Christ the solid Rock I stand,
All other ground is sinking sand;
All other ground is sinking sand.

-EDWARD MOTE

An inscription in his former church reads: "In loving memory of Mr. Edward Mote, who fell asleep in Jesus November 13, 1874, aged 77 years. For 26 years the beloved pastor of this church, preaching Christ and Him crucified, as all the sinner can need, and all the saint desire."

ON WINGS LIKE EAGLES

Those who wait on the LORD shall renew their strength;
They shall mount up with wings like eagles, they shall run and not be
weary, they shall walk and not faint.

ISAIAH 40:31 NKJV

Are you tired and disappointed? Are you feeling hopeless and scared? Now is the time to give up those feelings, turn to God, and allow Him to carry you. Andrew Murray compares God's relationship with us to a mother eagle teaching her young to fly.

You know how the eagles are taught the use of their wings. Picture a cliff rising a thousand feet out of the sea. See high up a ledge on the rock, where there is an eagle's nest with two young eaglets.

See the mother bird come and stir up her nest, and with her beak push the timid birds over the cliff. See how they flutter and fall and sink toward the bottom. See now how she flutters over her young, spreads wide her wings, and takes and bears them on her wings. (See Deuteronomy 32:11.) And so, she does once and again, each time casting them out over the cliff, and then taking and carrying them. The instinct of that eagle mother is God's gift, a single ray of that love in which the Almighty trains His people to mount as on eagles' wings.

He stirs up your nest. He disappoints your hopes. He brings

down your confidence. He makes you fear and tremble, as all your strength fails, and you feel utterly weary and helpless. And, all the while He is spreading His strong wings for you to rest your weakness on, and offering His everlasting strength to work in you. And all He asks is that you sink down in your weariness and wait on Him.

Allow Him in His strength to carry you as you ride on the wings of His omnipotence.

-ANDREW MURRAY

HOPE IN A LOVELY GOD

*You are fairer than the sons of men; Grace is poured upon Your lips;
Therefore God has blessed You forever.*

The book of Song of Songs in the Bible was written as a poetic
metaphor. Simply, it is a love poem about a woman and a man who
meet each other, sing praises about each other, and then get married, enjoy each other, and then joyfully sing some more praises. It
can also be read as a love story between the Church and Christ. It is
a passionate book, and when we read what the man says to his
beloved as what Christ says to us, it can be transforming.

God is simply amazing. That He is powerful, wise, gentle, and
good, and that He loves and adores us is hard to grasp. The
English Puritan John Flavel's following study on Song of Songs
focuses on the glorious loveliness that is our beloved Christ. He is
our hope and our salvation.

In Song of Songs chapter five, there is a question by the
daughters of Jerusalem, "What is your beloved more than another
beloved?" (v. 9 NKJV). The spouse answers, "He is the chief among
ten thousand." She then recounts many of the things she finds so
excellent in her beloved and then concludes with these words:
"Yes, he is altogether lovely" (v. 16 NKJV).

Christ is altogether lovely, the every part to be desired. He is
lovely when taken together, and in every part. It is as if she had

said, "Look on Him in what respect or particular you wish; cast your eye upon this lovely object, and view Him any way, turn Him in your serious thoughts whatever way you wish; consider His person, His positions, His works, or any other thing belonging to Him; you will find Him altogether lovely. There is nothing disagreeable in Him, there is nothing lovely without Him."

-JOHN FLAVEL

The Living Hope is our love, our Christ. And the amazing conclusion is that we will be in heaven, perfect, with Him.

Christ also loved the church and gave Himself up for her,
so that He might sanctify her, having cleansed her by the
washing of water with the word, that He might present to Himself
the church in all her glory, having no spot or wrinkle or any such thing;
but that she would be holy and blameless.

EPHESIANS 5:25-27 NASB

OPPORTUNITIES FOR GROWTH

*Consider it a sheer gift, friends, when tests and challenges come at you
from all sides. You know that under pressure, your faith-life is forced into
the open and shows its true colors. So don't try to get out of anything pre-
maturely. Let it do its work so you become mature and well-developed,
not deficient in any way.*

JAMES 1:2-4 MSG

When problems face us, what is our first response?
Frustration, annoyance, fear? Even if we calmly start problem-
solving, we are missing a great opportunity. James says we should
consider trials with joy. Of course, we don't typically say, "Wow,
thanks, God, my car broke down again. Here's another chance for
me to rely on You and grow."

It is hard to imagine that problems and trials have a purpose
in our lives. We tend to think they come directly from Satan and
cannot benefit us in the least. But God can use anything negative
in our lives to bless us and those around us. George Müller
explains that problems will push us to depend on God and will
ultimately help us grow stronger and wiser.

If we desire our faith to be strengthened, we should not
shrink from opportunities where our faith may be tested, and
through the test, be strengthened. In our natural state as sinners,
we dislike dealing with God alone. Through our natural alien-
ation from God we shrink from Him, and from spiritual truths.

Even as believers, we have the same shrinking from standing with God alone, from depending upon Him alone, and from looking to Him alone. Yet this is the very place where we should be for our faith to be strengthened. The more we are in a position to be tested in faith in the areas of our family, our physical body, our service for the LORD, our business, et cetera, the more we shall have opportunity of seeing God's help and deliverance. Each new instance where He helps and delivers us will tend to increase our faith more.

Therefore we shouldn't turn from situations, positions, and circumstances, where our faith may be tested. But we should cheerfully embrace them as opportunities where we may see the hand of God stretched out on our behalf, to help and deliver us. And our faith will be strengthened.

-GEORGE MÜLLER

O God, we sure don't like trials. They scare us and destroy our illusion that we are in control of our lives. We thank You that You are always in control. We are safe in Your hands. Shower us with Your peace as we face trials and remind us that You won't leave us to face them alone. Amen.

THROUGH FAITH BY GRACE

It is by grace you have been saved, through faith.

EPHESIANS 2:8 NIV

As Christians, we need faith, but our faith itself doesn't save us. It is God's grace that saves us through forgiveness, power, and love. Our faith simply believes and accepts God's amazing gifts. For example, if someone believed in the power of electricity to warm their house, it wouldn't be their strong belief that changed the temperature; it would be the actual electricity. But without their belief, they wouldn't hire someone to install the wiring or set the thermostat. Their belief allows them to access and use the power of electricity in their life.

This is how our faith in God allows His grace to bless the different areas of our lives. Charles Spurgeon gives several metaphors to explain the relationship between our faith and God's grace.

Grace is the first and last active cause of salvation. Faith, essential as it is, is only an important part of the machinery which grace uses. We are saved "through faith," but salvation is "by grace."

Faith occupies the position of a channel or conduit pipe. Grace is the fountain and the stream; faith is the aqueduct along which the flood of mercy flows down to refresh the thirsty people. It is a great pity when the aqueduct is broken. It is a sad sight to see around Rome the many great aqueducts which no longer convey water into the city, because the arches are broken and the marvelous structures are in ruins. The aqueduct must be kept entire to convey the current; and, even so, faith must be true and sound, leading right up to God and coming right down to ourselves, that it may become a serviceable channel of mercy to our souls.

Still, I again remind you that faith is only the channel or pipe, and not the fountainhead. We must not look so much to it or exalt it above the divine source of all blessing which lies in the grace of God. Never make a Christ out of your faith, nor think of faith as if it were the independent source of your salvation. Our life is found in "looking to Jesus," not in looking to our own faith.

By faith all things become possible to us; yet the power is not in the faith, but in the God upon whom faith relies. Grace is the powerful engine, and faith is the chain by which the soul is attached to the great motor power. The righteousness of faith is not the moral excellence of faith, but the righteousness of Jesus Christ which faith grasps and uses. The peace within the soul is not derived from the contemplation of our own faith; but it comes to us from Him who is our peace.

Therefore, the weakness of your faith will not destroy you. A trembling hand may receive a golden gift. The LORD's salvation can come to us though we have only faith as a grain of mustard seed. The power lies in the grace of God.

-CHARLES SPURGEON

The next time you worry about the future, about your faith,

or about God's willingness to bless you and answer your prayer, repeat the phrase, "A trembling hand may receive a golden gift." It is not by your strength that you are saved, nor by your worth that God continues to bless your life. It is only through God's love and grace that He blesses us, spends time with us, and changes us to become more like Him each day we spend with Him.

GRACE IN PRAYER

[Jesus] told me [Paul], "My grace is enough; it's all you need. My strength comes into its own in your weakness."

2 CORINTHIANS 12:9 MSG

Often we as Christians feel that we can't go to God with our little problems. Either God is too busy and doesn't care, or we feel we need to be more "spiritual" in our time with Him. How can we, as humans, bring our measly little problems to God? We should only come to Him for our big problems, and then only if we've been good!

Satan would like to convince us that we should only bring to God important things—our soul, the salvation of our friends and family, missionaries overseas. In this way we slowly begin to feel that God doesn't care about us, and we lose the desire to pray.

But God does care about our little problems. Sure, Christ healed major illnesses and brought Lazarus and others back from the dead, but He also healed Peter's mother-in-law of a minor fever. (See John 11:43; Matthew 8:14-15.) God cares about the little details in our lives because He cares for us. Just the way we enjoy listening to our friends and family babble to us about the day's occurrences and the thoughts and worries they've had, God enjoys listening to us. He enjoys spending time with us.

He longs to hear about our problems and to give us His peace. Jesus says, "Come to Me, all who are weary and heavy-laden, and I will give you rest" (Matthew 11:28 NASB). Annie

Johnson Flint writes that God's grace is enough to handle both our little woes and our life-stopping grief.

> *His grace is great enough to meet the great things,*
> *The crashing waves that overwhelm the soul,*
> *The roaring winds that leave us stunned and breathless,*
> *The sudden storms beyond our life's control.*
> *His grace is great enough to meet the small things,*
> *The little pin-prick troubles that annoy,*
> *The insect worries, buzzing and persistent,*
> *The squeaking wheels that grate upon our joy.*
>
> -ANNIE JOHNSON FLINT

Since God's grace is sufficient, we don't have to worry about going to God with our problems too often. The only thing necessary is that we keep on praying after we bring God our requests, let Him change our hearts and our lives, and speak to us where we are. The more time we spend with God, the more we become like Him and the more we can turn our problems over to Him with trust and peace.

"Let a person begin in prayer where he or she is, and that means anywhere, with any problem, with any desire. The only condition is that we stay on in prayer until the little things give way to the big things."

-DOUGLAS STEERE

HOPE IN AN INHERITANCE FROM GOD

[The apostle Paul said,] "I pray also that the eyes of your heart may be enlightened in order that you may know the hope to which he has called you, the riches of his glorious inheritance."

EPHESIANS 1:18 NIV

If we are saving up for a big vacation, we don't worry or complain about having to work overtime or having to be disciplined to spend our money carefully. Instead, we look to the future with hope and anticipation. We work hard and plan for the joy ahead. It is the same when we work for our treasure in heaven. Instead of complaining or struggling to remain disciplined and good, we get excited and pore over our Bibles, reading up about our future with such an awesome God. John Bunyan compares our hope to the hope of an adopted prince, ready and willing to fight any battle necessary for his Father-King.

There was a king that adopted one to be his child, and clothed him with royal clothes, and promised him that if he would fight his father's battles and walk in his father's ways, he should eventually share in the father's kingdom. He has received the adoption and the king's clothes, but not yet his part in the kingdom. But now his hope of a share in that will make him fight the king's battles, and also walk the king's paths.

Yes, and though he may encounter many things that could

discourage him from continuing, still thoughts of the promised kingdom, and hopes to enjoy it, will make him fight his way through those difficulties. His future hopes will, therefore, usher the child into a personal possession and enjoyment of that inheritance.

Hope has a thick skin, and will endure many a blow; it will put on patience as a vestment, it will wade through a sea of blood, it will endure all things if it be of the right kind, for the joy that is set before it. Hence patience is called "patience of hope," because it is hope that makes the soul exercise patience and long-suffering under the cross, until the time comes to enjoy the crown.

-JOHN BUNYAN

Hope contains the amazing quality of joy in longsuffering. It is the only thing that can keep us going, because it tells us, "Yes, it is worth the wait. Yes, it is worth this pain! Yes, you can keep going, because the result is going to be awesome!"

GOD LOVES "NOBODIES"

Isn't it obvious that God deliberately chose men and women that the culture overlooks and exploits and abuses, chose these "nobodies" to expose the hollow pretensions of the "somebodies"? That makes it quite clear that none of you can get by with blowing your own horn before God.

1 CORINTHIANS 1:27-29 MSG

Christ was not a great leader that we remember because of His triumphant conquests and victories in the past. Instead, Christ was born in a stable, coming to earth as a poor carpenter's son from a backwater town. His followers were mostly fishermen and tax collectors and women, not famous leaders or scholars.

When Christ traveled and preached, He took time out to notice and help the nobodies. Christ healed those who were unclean and couldn't go into the temple to worship. He blessed the little children who were brought to Him. He fetched water and talked to an adulterous Samaritan woman at the well, revealing to her that He indeed was the Christ. He spent time teaching and eating with the outcast tax collectors and sinners. He even washed the feet of His followers.

And finally, instead of rescuing His people from the Roman occupation and then triumphantly ruling as king, Jesus died a horrible, embarrassing death on the cross. Even His closest friends weren't expecting that climax, even though He warned them it was coming more than once. When Christ rose again, the first person who saw Him alive again was Mary Magdalene, who in Jewish society wasn't even a credible witness.

Jesus' actions on earth demonstrate God's love for everyone, especially the nobodies who need love and who are all alone. As a Shepherd, He leaves the ninety-nine healthy and safe sheep, and searches for the one scared and lost lamb. This shouldn't make us feel guilty or unworthy, but loved and cherished. We can be sure of two things: of our weakness and of His great grace and love for us.

God indeed loves nobodies. He seeks them out and tells them, "I made you, I know you, and I care for you."

GOD wasn't attracted to you and didn't choose you because you were big and important—the fact is, there was almost nothing to you.

DEUTERONOMY 7:7 MSG

GRACE MAKES
US BRAND-NEW

[Jesus said,] "That which is born of the flesh is flesh,
and that which is born of the Spirit is spirit.
Do not be amazed that I said to you,
'You must be born again.'"

JOHN 3:6-7 NASB

To truly be children of God and heirs to His kingdom, we must be born again, or made new. God's grace transforms us from slaves of sin to willing and happy slaves of love. Charles Spurgeon uses the example of a cat and a pig to show how we must be transformed if we are to act like saints.

Do you see that cat? What a clean creature it is! How cleverly it washes itself with its tongue and paws! It is quite a pretty sight! Did you ever see a pig do that? No, you never did. It is contrary to its nature. It prefers to wallow in the mud.

Go and teach a pig to wash itself, and see how little success you would have. Teach it to wash and clean itself as the cat has been doing! Useless task. You may wash that pig by force, but it hurries back to the mud and is soon as dirty as ever.

The only way in which you can get a pig to wash itself is to transform it into a cat; then it will wash and be clean, but not until then! And once that transformation is accomplished, then what was difficult or impossible is now easy. The swine will then be fit for your living room and your sofa.

So it is with an ungodly person. You cannot force them to do what a renewed person does most willingly. You may teach them, and set them a good example, but they cannot learn the art of holiness. Their nature leads them another way.

When the LORD makes a new person of them, then all things wear a different feature. So great is this change that I once heard a convert say, "Either the whole world is changed, or else I am." The new nature follows after right as naturally as the old nature wanders after wrong. What a blessing to receive such a nature!

The LORD's working in this matter is a great mystery: the Holy Spirit performs it. He who made the promise has the responsibility of keeping the promise, and He is able to handle it. God, who promises this marvelous change, will assuredly carry it out in all who receive Jesus, for to all such He gives power to become the Heirs of God.

-CHARLES SPURGEON

We cannot try to be holy saints anymore than a pig can try to be a cat. God must change us and then give us His power through His Holy Spirit that will continue to work through our lives. Our only job is to turn to God and ask Him to forgive us and to transform us by His saving grace.

If you are living according to the flesh, you must die;
but if by the Spirit you are putting to death the deeds of the body,
you will live. For all who are being led by the Spirit of God,
these are sons of God.

Romans 8:13-14 NASB

A Present and Future Hope

"I know the plans I have for you," declares the LORD, "plans to prosper
you and not to harm you, plans to give you hope and a future."

JEREMIAH 29:11 NIV

Faith in God is simply holding tightly to the assurance that
God is good, that God is in control, that God loves us, and that
in spite of circumstances, He will bless us. Christian faith is nothing without the encouraging buoy of hope that keeps us afloat
despite problems and pain.

God promises to "prosper" us and give us "hope and a future."
And by hope, He doesn't mean an empty hope, but one that will
be fulfilled. God does not break His promises. Philip Yancey says,
"Hope means simply the belief that something good lies ahead. It
is not the same as optimism or wishful thinking, for these imply a
denial of reality."

We as Christians aren't blind optimists unaware of the evil
and pain in the world. We are aware and we suffer, but our hope
and our energy comes from God. We know that He blesses us
during and after our pain. We know that He suffered when His
friends were sick and when He died on the cross. He alone has
comfort for us, and this comfort we can give to others.

When we become Christians, God doesn't promise us a
future without problems. In fact, Christ promises trials and tribu-
lations. (See John 16:33.) But He does ask us to come to Him
with our problems, and He assures us that He will comfort us

and bless us. (See 1 Peter 5:7; Matthew 11:28.) And as He comforts us, we will have the understanding to comfort others. The Christian editor and writer Mary Lou Redding said that it is our hope that pulls us along and lets us help others.

Our hope in God pulls us into the future. Hope allows us to affirm the reality of the abundant life that is ours in Christ. Hope allows us to stand with those in pain and to hold them until they are able to feel the love of God for themselves again. Hope allows us to work to bring God's reign upon the earth even when we see no results. Our hope begins and ends in God, the source of all hope.

-MARY LOU REDDING

When our faith is in a God who lovingly controls the future, our hope will be strong and will give us courage to face the worst.

GRACE SUFFICIENT FOR TODAY

[Jesus] said to me [Paul], "My grace is sufficient for you."

2 CORINTHIANS 12:9 NKJV

In the late nineteenth and the early twentieth century, Annie Johnson Flint encouraged thousands with her poems and letters. But the power of her words came from her personal experience with God's grace and mercy. From her early twenties, she suffered with crippling arthritis and remained bedridden the rest of her life. In spite of, or perhaps because of, her struggles, Flint's life was filled with the love of Christ.

The following portion of the Annie Johnson Flint poem, "One Day at a Time," reflects on the frustration and weariness we can face in one day and the strength and hope that Christ will give us to make it through.

> *One day at a time—but the day is so long,*
> *And the heart is not brave, and the soul is not strong,*
> *O Thou pitiful Christ, be Thou near all the way;*
> *Give courage and patience and strength for the day.*
>
> *Swift cometh His answer, so clear and so sweet;*
> *"Yea, I will be with thee, thy troubles to meet;*
> *I will not forget thee, nor fail thee, nor grieve;*
> *I will not forsake thee; I never will leave."*

Not yesterday's load we are called on to bear,
Nor the morrow's uncertain and shadowy care;
Why should we look forward or back with dismay?
Our needs, as our mercies, are but for the day.

One day at a time, and the day is His day;
He hath numbered its hours, though they haste or delay.
His grace is sufficient; we walk not alone;
As the day, so the strength that He giveth His own.

-ANNIE JOHNSON FLINT

God's grace and provision are sufficient for each day. He gave the Israelites enough manna for only one day at a time. (See Exodus 16:14-21.) And He will give us what we need to face our problems and to keep going each day. But most of all, God will be with us in the midst of our troubles. He will hold our hand and comfort us. "I can do all things through Christ who strengthens me" (Philippians 4:13 NKJV).

GOD IS ENOUGH

You keep me going when times are tough—my bedrock,
God, since my childhood.

PSALM 71:5 MSG

Consider these words by Hannah Whitall Smith:

We say sometimes, "If I could only find a promise to fit my case, I could then be at rest." But promises may be misunderstood or misapplied, and, at the moment when we are leaning all our weight upon them, they may seem utterly to fail us. But the Promiser, who is behind His promises and is infinitely more than His promises, can never fail nor change.

A little child does not need to have any promises from its mother to make it content; it has its mother herself, and she is enough. Its mother is better than a thousand promises. In our highest ideal of love or friendship, promises do not enter. One party may love to make promises, just as our LORD does, but the other party does not need them; the personality of lover or friend is better than all their promises.

Should every promise be wiped out of the Bible, we would still have God left, and God would be enough. Again I repeat it, only God, He Himself, just as He is, without the addition of anything on our part, whether it be disposition or feelings or experiences or good works or sound doctrines or any other thing either outward or inward. "He only is my rock and my salvation; He is my defense; I shall not be greatly moved" (Psalm 62:2 NKJV).

My own experience as a child taught me this, beyond any possibility of question. My mother was the remedy for all my own problems, and, I fully believed, for the problems of the whole world, if only they could be brought to her. And when anyone expressed doubts as to her ability to remedy everything, I remembered with what fine scorn I used to annihilate them, by saying, "Ah! but you don't know my mother."

And now, when any storm-tossed soul fails to see that God is enough, I feel like saying, not with scorn, but with infinite pity, "Ah, dear friend, you do not know God! If you knew Him, you could not help seeing that He is the remedy for every need of your soul, and that He is an all-sufficient remedy.

"God is enough, even though no promise may seem to fit your case, nor any inward assurance give you confidence. The Promiser is more than His promises; and His existence is a surer ground of confidence than the most fervent inward feelings."

-HANNAH WHITALL SMITH

"God is enough. God alone. If I have all else my heart would desire, and have not Him, I have nothing. If I have Him and nothing more, I have everything."

-RON MARR

ENDNOTES

1. This material is taken from *Making All Things New* by Oswald Chambers. Copyright © 1930, 1990 by the Oswald Chambers Publications Assoc. Ltd. and is used by permission of Discovery House Publishers, Box 3966, Grand Rapids, MI 49501. All rights reserved.

Additional copies of this and other products from Honor Books are available from your local bookseller.

The following titles are also available in this series:
Water from the Rock, Classic Edition
Water from the Rock, African-American Edition
Water from the Rock, Meditations on Peace and Purpose

If you have enjoyed this book,
or if it has had an impact on your life,
we would like to hear from you.

Please contact us at:
Honor Books, Dept. 201
4050 Lee Vance View
Colorado Springs, CO 80918
Or visit our Web site:
www.cookministries.com

HONOR HB BOOKS
Inspiration and Motivation for the Seasons of Life